Living with hardship 24/7:

The diverse experiences of families in poverty in England

Carol-Ann Hooper, Sarah Gorin, Christie Cabral and Claire Dyson

The Frank Buttle Trust
Audley House, 13 Palace Street, London SW1E 5HX
www.buttletrust.org

© The Frank Buttle Trust 2007

First published in 2007 by The Frank Buttle Trust

ISBN: 978 0 9555614 0 5

All rights reserved.

Carol-Ann Hooper, Sarah Gorin, Christie Cabral and Claire Dyson
assert the moral right to be identified as the authors of this work.

British Library Cataloguing in Publication Data:
A catalogue record for this publication is available from the British Library

Cover design by yo-yo.uk.com, York

Prepared and printed by:
York Publishing Services Ltd
64 Hallfield Road, Layerthorpe, York YO31 7ZQ
Tel: 01904 431213   Fax: 01904 430868   Website: www.yps-publishing.co.uk

Contents

For the families who entrusted us with their stories

Foreword

by The Rt. Hon. Gordon Brown, MP
Prime Minister

I was very pleased to be asked to write the foreword to this research report, which graphically highlights the experiences of parents and children living in poverty in England today and makes recommendations as to how service provision for families can be made in a more holistic and effective way.

The Government pledged in 1999 to halve child poverty by 2010 and to end it by 2020. While absolute poverty in Britain has fallen as a result of the measures taken by the Government, there are still 2.8 million children living in poverty in the UK today – that is one in three children. A great deal more needs to be done.

The Government is, and I personally am, committed to giving every child the opportunity to achieve their full potential. That is the way forward for the attainment of individual achievement and happiness, and for the prosperity of society as a whole. This research report provides valuable signposts for all agencies with responsibility for children's well-being to work strategically together to maximise the beneficial impact of their services on children and families.

I commend The Frank Buttle Trust, not just for its outstanding grant-aid work, supporting individual children, young people and families living in poverty, but for its commitment to making a lasting change, by commissioning this research to highlight the impact of poverty on the lives of children and their parents. All agencies that play a role in the lives of these families need to take note of the findings and recommendations of this report.

Gordon Brown

Acknowledgements

We would like to thank first and foremost all the families (and the children, women and men within them) who generously invited us into their lives, gave us their time and shared their experiences with us.

We are grateful also to the local authority social services departments, schools and voluntary organisations that helped us make contact with families; to the social workers, health visitors and teachers who took time out of pressured working days to participate in focus group discussions; to our colleagues at the NSPCC and University of York for their comments and feedback; to Alanna Ivin at Rapid Transcriptions and Sara Christianson for their hard work transcribing the interviews; and to Nazma Jalil for translation and interpretation support.

The Frank Buttle Trust, the NSPCC and the University of York, working in partnership, developed the research on which this report is based. The research project was funded by the Big Lottery Fund, and The Frank Buttle Trust, the NSPCC and the University of York also contributed staff time to the project.

The Frank Buttle Trust would like to thank Sir Richard Tilt for chairing the Advisory Group, and all of the members for their enthusiasm, active participation, expertise and sound advice.

THE ADVISORY GROUP

Mary Armitage, Child Protection Officer, Education Leeds
Prof. Jonathan Bradshaw, Department of Social Policy and Social Work, University of York
David Coulter, Senior Policy Adviser, NSPCC
Alan Darke, Casework Manager, The Frank Buttle Trust
Matt Davies, ATD Fourth World
Paul Dornan, Head of Policy, CPAG
Prof. Brid Featherstone, Social Sciences and Humanities, University of Bradford
Bodil Mlynarska, Child Protection, Camden Social Services
Hilary Paxman, Department for Communities and Local Government
Honor Rhodes, Coram Family
Karen Woodall, Chief Executive, Centre for Separated Families
Prof. Ian Sinclair, Social Work Research and Development Unit, University of York
Sir Richard Tilt, Independent Review Service
Dot Yellen, Development Manager, NSPCC Services for Children and Young People

1 Introduction: why another study on parenting in poverty?

The Labour government pledged in 1999 to end child poverty by 2020. Significant progress has been made towards that end – the number of children in poverty has declined by 23 per cent since 1998/99. Despite this, the proportion of children living in poverty in the UK remains higher than it was a generation ago and higher than in most European countries (Harker, 2006; Hirsch, 2006). Children who grow up in poverty are at increased risk of a wide range of adverse experiences and negative outcomes, including poor health (physical and mental), death from illness or accident, educational disadvantage and disaffection, physical abuse and neglect by parents, victimisation by crime, and criminalisation for anti-social behaviour or offending. Their disadvantage may persist well into adult life, with low aspirations as well as accumulated disadvantage creating an increased risk of unemployment, low pay and poverty as adults. There is no evidence that such negative long-term impacts are diminishing – on the contrary, they were greater for children who grew up poor in the 1980s than for those who grew up poor in the 1970s (Hirsch, 2006).

Poverty experts, including an independent adviser appointed by the government (Harker, 2006), urge more radical action to meet the government's pledge. At the same time, the new duty that local authorities have under the Children Act 2004 to work in partnership with other services to promote children's well-being reflects higher aspirations and a shift towards greater social responsibility for children. This report, based on qualitative research with 70 low-income families and with professionals who work with such families, aims to contribute to the efforts ongoing in many contexts to make that vision a reality.

THE STUDY

The research project was originally conceived in 2000. It was funded for two years, 2004–06, and the fieldwork was conducted in 2005–06. Its focus evolved over time – from an initial interest in understanding better the known association between poverty and the risk of some forms of child maltreatment (physical abuse and neglect), towards a broader concern with the complex relationships between poverty, parenting and children's well-being in diverse social circumstances. The relevant literature has grown significantly over the period, including reviews of the literature on parenting in poverty (Attree, 2004; Katz *et al.*, 2007, forthcoming) and new research studies (see especially Ghate and Hazel, 2002; Seaman *et al.*, 2005; CSCI, 2006).

This project remains unique in three main ways, however.

- First, the sample was constructed to enable exploration of the diversity of experience among families in poverty. It includes families living on a low income in areas of high socio-economic deprivation and also areas of relative affluence, and families from a range of ethnic backgrounds (including nine Bangladeshi families). Since families were contacted via schools, social services departments (including some families with children on the Child Protection Register) and voluntary organisations, it includes families with a range of different troubles and experiences of services.

- Second, a depth of understanding of families' lives was made possible by covering parents' life histories as well as their current circumstances, social networks and experience of services, and by interviewing both parents (where there were two) and one child where possible.

- Third, the interviews covered participants' experience of a wide range of services, rather than a single service or part of a service, as is common in research on 'user views'.

The report therefore captures much of the quality of the relationship between low-income families and the state in Britain today, and goes both broader and deeper than previous research in understanding their lives. At a time of rapid development of services, and increasing recognition of the need for a holistic approach to intervention and support for families (CSCI, 2006; HM Government, 2006a), it offers a valuable perspective from the inside.

THE CONTEXT – KEY CONCEPTS AND ISSUES

POVERTY, INEQUALITY AND SOCIAL EXCLUSION

The project was entitled 'Parenting on a low income: stress, support and children's well-being'. We did not use the term poverty in any publicity for the project, as we anticipated (rightly) that some of the people we wished to interview would not want to identify themselves in this way, for a range of reasons (largely the stigma and shame attached to poverty and/or differences of definition). Nevertheless, by the definitions of poverty most commonly used in the UK - either those in receipt of means-tested benefits or with below 60 per cent of median income before housing costs – the vast majority of the households we interviewed were poor.[1]

 A relative definition of poverty, based on the impact of lack of resources on the ability to participate in the ordinary life of one's society, is now widely accepted in both academic and policy contexts in the UK[2] (though public support for it remains partial – Lister, 2004). By such definitions, around 700,000 children have been lifted out of poverty since 1997, to a large extent by encouraging more parents to work (with increased childcare provision and financial support through tax credits). Nevertheless, around 2.4 million children still live in poverty (DWP, 2006) and for many it is both severe and persistent. It is not inevitable that the presence of dependent children in the household significantly increases the risk of poverty, as it does in the UK. In the Nordic countries, where greater commitment to societal responsibility for children is reflected in greater state support for families, children are significantly less vulnerable to poverty than adults (Bradshaw, 2000; Lister, 2004).[3]

Poverty involves children and their parents (especially, often, their mothers) going without much that other people take for granted, and living with high levels of worry and uncertainty about how both anticipated and unanticipated expenses can be met. It also involves being positioned socially as outside the norms that most people take for granted, in terms of the choices promoted in a consumer society and the capacities needed to participate in it. This social positioning affects many everyday encounters between 'the poor' and others, both in local communities and in service contexts, and experiences of stigma, disrespect and lack of recognition of equal human worth are common. These different dimensions of poverty are what Lister (2004) refers to in her conceptualisation of poverty as a wheel, as the material core (a condition of disadvantage and insecurity), and the equally important hub of social relations, in which 'the poor' are perceived as the devalued 'Other'. The social relations dimensions are as much about inequality as poverty, and inequality has an independent impact on well-being (Wilkinson, 2005). Whether people are happy with their income depends not only on its level but also on how that compares both with what they are used to and with what others around them have (Layard, 2005). Health tends to be better in more equal places, whether because happiness in turn affects health and/or because inequality has other effects on community life, undermining trust, mutual respect, participation and safety (Wilkinson, 2005).

Concerns with disadvantage are increasingly framed in policy debates around the concept of social exclusion. This captures some of the social relations dimensions of poverty, highlighting the institutional processes that may enable or inhibit participation in full citizenship, for example exclusion from the labour market, lack of access to public and private services, and social isolation. It also focuses on the way multiple disadvantages become concentrated in particular localities, where poverty may be accompanied by high levels of unemployment, educational disadvantage and disaffection, poor housing and crime.

There is much overlap between poverty and social exclusion, but the latter is a complex and multidimensional phenomenon, not confined to one clearly definable group. Individuals and households may be included on one dimension and excluded on another, the pattern influenced by such factors as age, health/disability, gender and ethnicity as well as locality. Much policy effort is currently focused on 'deprived neighbourhoods' in response to the recognition of spatial concentration – including such area-based initiatives (ABIs) as Sure Start. Both poverty and social exclusion clearly exist in other areas too, however, often alongside more visible local inequality. Taking seriously the social dimensions of poverty involves recognising the diversity of those contexts (both community and socio-cultural) and their consequences. This report aims to contribute to that recognition.

CHILD WELL-BEING, MALTREATMENT AND PARENTING IN POVERTY

Children's well-being is defined in England and Wales in terms of five dimensions:

- being healthy (including physical and mental health)

- staying safe (from maltreatment, bullying, victimisation by crime and other risks, e.g. accidents)

- enjoying and achieving (including educational attainment and leisure activities)

- making a positive contribution (avoiding anti-social behaviour and participation in e.g. voluntary activity)

- achieving economic well-being (in terms of both present household income and future earning potential).

All of these are influenced by poverty, among other factors. Parents also play a part in relation to them all, through their paid work and its influence on household resources, their involvement in community life and their parenting.

The extent to which negative outcomes for children living in poverty are the result of parenting practices or other poverty-related factors is unclear (Katz *et al.*, 2007, forthcoming). There are many other relevant factors – the quality of local schools and children's experiences within them, the accessibility and quality of other services, the opportunities for play in the area, the state of the neighbourhood environment, the involvement of local people in crime and drugs, and the availability of local jobs. These aspects of their social context all send messages to young people about their own value and the opportunities open to them. Research with children and young people has found that many report experiencing stigma, sadness, shame and a feeling of being different and inferior as a direct result of poverty (Crowley and Vulliamy, 2002; Ridge, 2002, Willow, 2002).

At the same time, poverty clearly impacts on parenting in a wide range of ways. The increased risk of physical abuse and neglect associated with poverty (Drake and Pandey, 1996; Gillham *et al.*, 1998; Cawson *et al.*, 2000; Sidebotham *et al.*, 2002; Sidebotham and Heron, 2006) is one of these. We addressed this issue explicitly (by both the sampling method and the interview topics) in order to increase understanding of the association. Our intention in doing so is emphatically *not* to pathologise poor parents as people who parent poorly. That equation is too easily made and should be avoided. Many parents do a remarkable job despite (often multiple) adverse circumstances and the vast majority of parents living in poverty do not maltreat their children. Nor is it to reduce the problem of maltreatment to poverty, as it has sometimes been in the past. All forms of maltreatment occur across socio-economic groups and poverty is only one of many factors that may contribute. But children themselves say 'staying safe' is the most important of the child well-being outcomes (Jewell, 2006; Madge, 2006), and there is growing concern that the increased vulnerability of children living in poverty to some forms of maltreatment may play a part in the passing on of disadvantage from generation to generation (Lovell, 1992; Katz, 2004; Katz *et al.*, 2007, forthcoming). Children who experience both poverty and maltreatment are likely to be doubly disadvantaged, although it is difficult to separate the impacts of one experience from the other where they are closely interwoven.

There is already a vast literature on risk and resilience factors affecting outcomes for children, including the different forms of maltreatment. There is also a growing reliance on such research in the construction of tools for assessment, with the aim of predicting risk and targeting interventions accordingly to prevent poor outcomes. A qualitative study of this kind offers something rather different by exploring the stories behind the categories recognised to increase risk (e.g. parents' own histories of abuse, domestic violence or psychiatric history) or resilience (e.g. social support) and the processes involved in their influence.

For services to engage with parents for the well-being of children, the biographical contexts of their needs and their relevance to parents' own well-being, identity and parenting need to be recognised, without losing sight of the impact of the broader community, socio-economic and cultural contexts. Such a perspective is essentially the 'ecological model'[4] for assessing the needs of children and families now embedded in policy guidance (Department of Health, Department for Education and Employment and Home Office, 2000). While large-scale quantitative studies are necessary for identifying 'risk factors' with some predictive power, qualitative research can offer more insight into the interactions between different levels of context and processes, and can therefore help to develop anti-oppressive practice.

RETHINKING SERVICES FOR CHILDREN AND FAMILIES

The framework of intended outcomes for children's well-being was developed by the Children and Young People's Unit in consultation with children and young people, parents/ carers and professionals working with children. It is a central plank of the vision set out in *Every Child Matters* (HM Government, 2004) for every child, whatever their background or circumstances. Among other things, it means that, for the first time, agencies in effect have a duty directly to prevent maltreatment,[5] rather than – as in previous legislation – simply to prevent children's reception into care or appearance at juvenile court (the Children and Young Persons Act 1963) or to promote their upbringing within their families (the Children Act 1989). That duty applies to all children, not only those who come into contact with social services departments (or children's services departments as they are gradually being redesignated). Local authorities and other key agencies in each area must now produce a Children and Young People's Plan (in most cases annually) based on identifying where outcomes on the five dimensions of well-being need to be improved and how that improvement will be achieved.

Developments in services prompted by the new duty to promote children's well-being are occurring in the context of much change, both organisational and technological. At national level, most responsibilities for children have now been brought together in one central government department, the Department for Education and Skills (DfES), to promote a more coordinated and joined-up approach to services for children and families. At local level, children's trusts are being established as the new framework for partnership between different agencies, with social services and education being combined under the leadership of new directors of children's services, and a range of different local arrangements for the involvement of other agencies. Records of assessments conducted by social services with children and families are increasingly computerised under the Integrated Children's System. A new computerised information-sharing index to cover all children has also been announced (to be operational by the end of 2008) to enable practitioners to communicate their concerns about a child more easily, and to facilitate early intervention to promote children's well-being. These developments were influenced by the inquiry into Victoria Climbié's death and the failures of communication between and within agencies that it identified. They also reflect a broader agenda of investing in children as the future – as Gordon Brown put it, 'children are 20 per cent of the population but they are 100 per cent of the future'. This is a long-standing theme in social policy, re-emphasised and reshaped by the current government, partly in the light of a shift in thinking about the welfare state (towards a 'social investment' model)[6] and partly to reflect concerns with preventing social exclusion.

Initiatives focusing on children, young people, parents and/or families have proliferated since 1997, many of them multi-agency (often involving both statutory and voluntary organisations) and focused on deprived areas. Those that are now well established include Sure Start (multi-agency projects initially focusing on parents with pre-school children in deprived areas and now being extended into children's centres and being rolled out to all areas by 2010), the Children's Fund (funding for the voluntary sector to provide services to support children aged five to 13), Connexions (offering advice, support and information to older young people aged 13 to 19) and a range of initiatives under the remit of the Home Office or Youth Justice Board that are intended to reduce the risk of offending by young people. A Parenting Fund has now been added to support voluntary organisations working with parents (HM Treasury/DfES, 2005) and a number of intensive family intervention projects using a range of approaches, including full residential supervision and support where problems are particularly severe, are being rolled out (Home Office, 2006).

Recent developments are based on the principle of 'progressive universalism' (HM Treasury/DfES, 2005), i.e. embedding support for all within universal services, with access via those services to more targeted or specialist support. The development of extended schools, and the addition of a school-based outreach role, parent support advisers, to be piloted in primary and secondary schools (HM Treasury/DfES, 2005), reflect this principle. So, too, do health-led parenting support demonstration projects, involving nurses visiting mothers from before the birth of a child for the child's first two years (HM Government, 2006a). Such developments make it important to understand how parents experience not only specific interventions but also their broader interaction with different institutions.

It is a time of rapid and major change, with the map of services for children and families an increasingly complex and diverse one. The intention now is clearly to move from a reactive approach, responding only to families in crisis, to a more preventative one – a welcome shift *if* it is matched by sufficient resources (CSCI, 2006; HM Government, 2006b). Interventions whose aims are defined in rather vague 'preventative' terms may have a range of different purposes however, influenced by the priorities of the organisation within which the service sits, as well as the broader policy agenda on social exclusion. Their goals may include supporting parents and enhancing children's well-being, often alongside reinforcing parents' responsibilities either to work or in relation to their children, and their children's responsibilities to become responsible citizens in the future. The linking of rights to responsibilities is another key New Labour theme, with the balance between them an important influence on families' experience of services, as is the extent to which rights are matched by the resources to make them a reality.

Consultation with children and parents as users of services increasingly informs policy developments at national and local level. Qualitative research can give much more depth of understanding of 'user views' than is gained by most such consultations, however, although the interpretation of accounts requires care and sensitivity to the context in which they are expressed.

THE REPORT

The project on which this report is based was commissioned by The Frank Buttle Trust and funded by the Big Lottery Fund. The next chapter describes the methods used and the sample it is based on. Chapters 3–6 report its findings. Chapter 3 focuses first on common themes in the families' experiences of poverty and then explores the influence of diversity of community and socio-cultural contexts. Chapter 4 draws on the life histories of the parents to explore the way the stresses of parenting in poverty are interwoven with other experiences of adversity and the influence of these on parents' sources of support. Chapter 5 focuses on the children's experience, drawing on interviews both with them and with their parents. The many ways in which poverty is relevant to children's well-being are summarised here (pp. 68–69). Chapter 6 discusses the role of services in promoting social inclusion or perpetuating social exclusion. Chapter 7 draws on the previous chapters and uses case studies to reflect on the known association between poverty and some forms of maltreatment. Chapter 8 reflects on directions in current policy in the light of our findings and makes recommendations for specific services.

NOTES

1. According to the information we gathered about household income and benefits received, eight households had equivalised incomes above the poverty threshold of 60 per cent median income before housing costs. For five of these, this was because they received disability-related benefits (disabled living allowance or carer's allowance), and the extra income is therefore a reflection of extra needs. Of the three others, one had an income just above the threshold, the two others an income around £50 per week over it.

2. Townsend's (1979) definition still expresses this approach well: 'Individuals, families and groups can be said to be in poverty if they lack the resources to obtain the types of diet, participate in the activities and have the living conditions and amenities which are customary, or at least widely encouraged or approved in the societies to which they belong'.

3. In a recent comparison, child poverty rates in Norway, Sweden, Finland and Denmark are recorded as below 5 per cent, compared to 15.4 per cent in the UK (Unicef, 2005).

4. The ecological model was devised by Bronfenbrenner (1979). Essentially it refers to locating an understanding of children and the risks to their well-being and development (including the risk of maltreatment) within the multiple interrelated contexts of their relationships with their carers, their home and wider family networks, their schools, their local communities and the broader cultural, social and economic contexts.

5. This is not the wording of the legislation but in our view it is the logic of the duty placed on children's services authorities to cooperate to safeguard and improve children's well-being.

6. The 'social investment' state is a term coined by Giddens (1998) to refer to the shift in the perceived aims of welfare, from offering protection from the market, towards facilitating integration into the market, through investment in 'human capital' wherever possible.

2 *Methodology and sample*

The overall aim of this research project was to explore in depth the relationships between poverty, parenting and children's well-being, in diverse social contexts, from the perspectives of parents, children and professionals. More specifically, it explored:

- parents' perceptions of the impacts of living on a low income on their own lives and well-being, their family relationships and their children's well-being, including any incidents of child maltreatment

- the experiences of parents living in poverty of a range of statutory and non-statutory services, both universal and more specialist or targeted services

- the possible influence of parents' own childhood and life experiences on their parenting, their access to and experience of social support and services, and the ways in which they cope with the stresses they experience

- children's perceptions of poverty and how it impacts on their lives, including how it affects their relationships with their parents and other family members

- professionals' perceptions of the impacts and relevance of poverty to the challenges of parenting, and of the adequacy of service responses to these.

DESCRIPTION OF METHODS

SAMPLE RECRUITMENT We wanted to compare the experience of low-income families living in areas with high levels of deprivation with the experience of low-income families living in affluent areas. We used the Indices of Multiple Deprivation (IMD) provided by the Office of National Statistics to identify local authorities (LAs) with high and low levels of deprivation close to the two research bases, one in London and one in York. In London, three LAs that had IMD ranks indicating they were in the 10 per cent most deprived in the country agreed to participate. In Yorkshire, two LAs with IMD ranks that put them in the 40 per cent least deprived in the country were identified; one agreed to participate and the other did not. Most of the families recruited were therefore from the former area (the more affluent of the two) but some families were also contacted in the latter via voluntary organisations.

The deprived LAs in London were characterised by below-average household income, high levels of unemployment, an ethnically diverse population and large numbers of low-income families. The less deprived LAs in the North of England had far fewer low-income families, and were predominantly white and much more affluent overall; most of the participating families lived in small towns or cities but a few lived in villages in the surrounding countryside.

We wanted our sample of families to encompass several dimensions of diversity in addition to coming from contrasting areas. We wanted to include both families in which child maltreatment had occurred and families in which it had not, families who had experienced different levels of intervention from social services or none at all, and families who had experienced a range of family support services from statutory and non-statutory bodies. We also wanted to include families with diverse ethnic backgrounds, in particular Bangladeshi families who are among the most vulnerable to poverty in the country (Lister, 2004), and at least some non-English-speaking Bangladeshi families. Finally, we wanted to interview families who had children young enough still to affect their parents' labour-market participation and to interview children aged between five to 11 years, as there has been little research with children of this age group on their perspectives on living in poverty. We restricted recruitment to families with at least one child in this age range.

We recruited low-income families[1] through social services, via voluntary organisations and through schools serving the same communities. The organisations sent families information about the research and an invitation to participate. Families could then 'opt in' to the research by contacting the research team. Information that went out to Bangladeshi families was sent in English and Bengali, and families who returned the Bengali reply slip were contacted by a Bengali-speaking interpreter who explained the research and the process to families before confirming whether they wished to participate. Families were given £30 in gift vouchers for a shop of their choice to thank them for their time.

The total sample was of 70 families, 32 living in areas of high deprivation and 38 in more affluent areas. Of the families recruited through voluntary organisations or schools, almost half had previously been in contact with social services (although not all had received support). Of the 70 families, 12 families had experience of children being placed on the Child Protection Register (CPR), 30 of receiving family support services via social services, nine had had contact with social services but no support (either they had been assessed and no further action had been taken or they had requested but had been refused assistance) and 19 families had had no contact with social services. Nine Bangladeshi families and a further 18 black and minority ethnic (BME) families, a few of whom were recent immigrants, participated in the research (for full sample description see the section headed 'Demographic information about the sample' later in this chapter).

THE RESEARCH PROCESS

Ideally, we wanted to interview both parents/caregivers[2] (where there were two) and the oldest child aged five to 11 in each household. However, not all resident partners agreed to be interviewed, a few parents refused permission for their children to be interviewed and, in one family, the father would only allow an interview with himself.

The adult interview schedule was semi-structured and used flexibly to allow exploration of issues as parents raised them. The interviews took an in-depth life history approach covering experiences of living on a low income, parenting, childhood and family relationships, past or current trauma or difficulties, social networks and service use. The interview involved the use of two standardised measures completed by parents: the Malaise Inventory (Rutter *et al.*, 1970) focusing on themselves and measuring adult stress; and the Strengths and Difficulties Questionnaire focusing on children, which gives several measures of behavioural difficulties (Goodman, 1997). The Parent–Child Relationship Questionnaire from Ghate and Hazel (2002) was used as a prompt to discussion of individual parent–child relationships within each family. The interview also included several survey-style checklists, which parents usually filled in themselves, some giving basic demographic information on the household members, one with questions relating to their attachment to their own parents (from a questionnaire devised by McCluskey, Heard and Lake, work in progress) and their self-esteem, three modified from Ghate and Hazel (2002) on parents' restrictions, past and current difficulties and their social networks, and one on the services used by parents.

The interview with caregivers typically took three to four hours but ranged from one to as much as five hours on occasion. An interpreter worked with the researcher in conducting interviews with Bengali-speaking Bangladeshi parents and these tended to take longer. All interviews were undertaken in families' homes and were normally recorded using a digital voice recorder. Several Bangladeshi families did not want the interview recorded and, in these cases, notes were taken during the interview and observations written up afterwards. Ideally, each family member was interviewed alone, but this was not always possible (because participants or families members were unwilling to allow this or because of space constraints in overcrowded housing). This meant that sensitive parts of interviews were sometimes addressed at a separate time and occasionally had to be partially omitted.

The interviews with children were designed to be playful and used a workbook with exercises for them to complete, ink stamps for them to use and pictures to colour in. Typically, children's interviews lasted 30 to 45 minutes. The researcher had a topic guide and used this and the workbook flexibly and responsively with the child. Topics covered children's social networks, their likes and dislikes at home and school, perceptions and experiences of living on a low income, perceptions of parental stress and aspirations for their current and future lives. They were asked if they felt safe at home and school and who with, and who they would go to if they needed help. Children were not asked directly about maltreatment or trauma but were able to speak about it if they raised it themselves. At the end of the interview, each child was given a small thank-you present.

In conducting and analysing the interviews, we were influenced by Hollway and Jefferson's (2000) perspective on the psycho-social subject in qualitative research, whose accounts need to be understood within the contexts of the person's biography, their cultural context and the intersubjective dynamics of the interview. We all tell and retell our stories differently at different times and investments in particular discursive positions – e.g. that of the good mother or father – may serve a defensive function against anxiety. Complex, conflicted and contradictory narratives are common in interviews about family life and the impacts of trauma – a feature of many of our participants' lives – and the sensitivity of some of the topics we covered could further undermine coherence. An approach to interviewing that allowed participants to tell their stories in their own way as far as possible was taken, while also probing to obtain as clear as possible an understanding of events and their impact, in order to maximise our ability to make sense of the accounts we gathered.

ETHICAL PROCEDURES   The sensitive nature of this project has meant that there were many ethical considerations to address. We developed an ethical protocol for the research and a policy on child protection that laid out the steps that would be taken should we have concerns about a child while undertaking fieldwork. The key principles of our protocol were safeguarding participants, ensuring informed consent throughout the process and protecting the confidentiality of participants. If child protection concerns were raised during contact with the family, these would be discussed initially with the parent, then with an independent child protection professional who would help researchers to identify circumstances of sufficient concern to justify breaching confidence. These would then be reported to social services, keeping the families informed of the action taken. Three such referrals were made during the course of the research. Ethical approval for the project was gained from an ethics committee at York University at the beginning of the project. Additionally, local ethics approval was gained from one local authority research governance board and from a local research ethics committee (LREC).

Informed consent was sought at several stages throughout the research process – at first contact (usually by phone) and at the beginning of each meeting with participants for first and subsequent interviews. Informed consent for the child's interview was sought from parents and from the child, and the interview did not take place if it was felt that the child could not give informed consent. At each stage, the research purpose and process were explained, with the assistance of an interpreter for Bengali-speaking families, including the protocol that would be followed should child safety concerns emerge. Both adults and children were talked through and asked to sign a written consent form at the beginning of their interviews.

Particular emphasis was placed on the voluntary nature of participation and participants were told that they did not have to answer all questions posed; they were reminded of this during interviews before sensitive issues were raised and at other times if they showed any sign of discomfort or distress. We were conscious of the power difference between the adult researcher and children being interviewed that might inhibit children from declining to participate or answer certain questions. In order to address this, a number of measures were taken. The children were given a red card and a green card to signify stop and go, and they could hold up a red card if they did not want to respond to a particular question (this was particularly useful with children of more limited verbal ability). Children were given control of the workbook and sometimes also the recorder so that they could turn a page if they wanted to stop discussing a topic or turn off the recorder if they wanted to say something 'off record'.

Any sign of discomfort or distress in the children was taken as a withdrawal of consent (whether or not they said anything or held up a red card) and the researcher would move on to the next topic or stop the interview altogether if the child continued to show signs of discomfort. Adults were given the option to stop or move to another topic if they became distressed during an interview but frequently chose to continue talking about circumstances that were invariably very significant parts of their life stories.

It was anticipated that the adult interviews could identify needs for help that were not within the role of the research interview itself to address (ranging from practical such as debt or financial management, to emotional such as experiences of trauma). Before starting interviews, researchers identified support organisations nationally and locally, and compiled this information into leaflets. These were given to participants at the end of interviews and researchers offered to help participants make contact with organisations that might be able to give them support; a few participants accepted this offer, mainly for practical assistance.

Feedback on the interview experience was sought from families about a month after the interviews had been completed (to allow some time for reflection). Forms for each participant, including one specially designed for the child, were sent to families with a return Freepost envelope. The feedback was very positive; adults frequently commented that they felt listened to, unjudged and able to tell their own stories as they wished, several commenting that this was the first opportunity they had had for doing so. Some also appeared to find participation empowering and said how glad they were to have had the opportunity to contribute their views and experiences to research that might influence policy. All names used to refer to participants in the report are fictional.

FOCUS GROUPS WITH PROFESSIONALS

Six focus groups of professionals, three in the deprived areas and three in the affluent areas, were recruited – in each context, one with a group of social workers and family support workers, the second with a group of teachers and the third with a group of health visitors. Each group met for about an hour-and-a-half and discussions were recorded to gather professionals' perspectives on the issues facing families living on a low income, the relationship between low income and parenting problems, the response of local services to families and any challenges, the effectiveness of multi-agency working for families on a low income and the impact of policy changes on provision of services. At the end of the analysis, a summary of findings was sent out to these groups and they were invited to comment and contribute to recommendations. Three groups (teachers and health visitors from deprived areas and social workers from affluent areas) met with researchers to give their feedback and the others sent feedback individually.

DEMOGRAPHIC INFORMATION ABOUT THE SAMPLE

The following section gives basic demographic and background information about the families interviewed for this research. The sample was obtained in a way that encompassed a wide range of experiences but was not statistically representative of low-income families in either area or of families receiving support from services. Therefore the statistics in this section are descriptive of the sample only and should not be extrapolated to a wider population. This description is given as context for the chapters that follow, which offer analysis of the data generated from this sample. While many of the themes from the families' accounts offer insights into processes relevant to the wider population of families living on a low income, the detailed description is given to enable the reader to bear in mind similarities and differences between our sample and other families.

AGE AND GENDER

In the 70 low-income households that participated in the study, interviews were carried out with 82 adults (including 15 men) and 59 children (of five to 11 years). The participating men had an older age range than the participating women (age and gender distributions were very similar for deprived and affluent areas) (Figure 2.1). Overall, a slightly higher number of girls (32) were interviewed than boys (27), the majority (68 per cent) in the eight to 11 years age range (Figure 2.1). The sample from more deprived areas had roughly equal numbers of girls and boys but the sample from more affluent areas had twice as many girls as boys. This is not because of any sampling bias, but simply because the families who agreed to participate had twice as many girls of the appropriate age as boys.

Figure 2.1: Age and gender of adults and children in sample

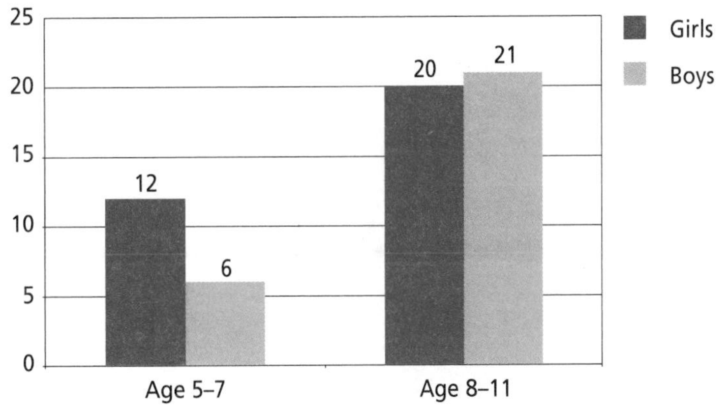

ETHNICITY Sample families from deprived areas were much more ethnically diverse than those from affluent areas – Bangladeshi was the most common ethnicity, followed by white British and smaller groups of black Caribbean and black African and a few of Other white, Asian and mixed ethnicities (Figure 2.2). The sample of children from more deprived areas followed a similar pattern, but with a larger proportion of mixed ethnicities (Figure 2.2). The sample from the affluent areas was almost entirely of white British ethnicity (95 per cent) with the remaining 5 per cent of adults giving their ethnicity as Other white. Similarly, 94 per cent of children in the affluent area were white British with just 2 per cent of mixed ethnicity (Figure 2.2).

There were 19 first-generation immigrants in the deprived areas sample, amounting to 49 per cent of adults interviewed in deprived areas, and one immigrant in the affluent area sample. Almost all had migrated to the UK as adults, most had been resident for four to 20 years and a few for over 30 years. Immigrants made up a large proportion or sometimes all of certain ethnic groups. All Bangladeshi except one man were immigrants, all those identifying themselves as of black African ethnicity were immigrants (one from each of Uganda, Nigeria, Somalia and Ethiopia). There was also a woman from Thailand, a man from Mauritius and (in the affluent area) a man from Turkey.

Figure 2.2: Ethnicity of adults and children in sample

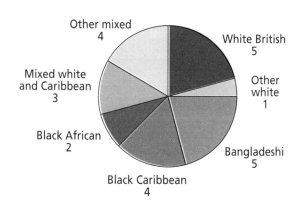

Number of adults in deprived areas

Number of children in deprived areas

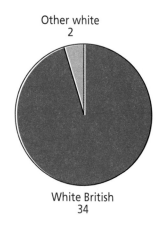

Number of adults in affluent areas

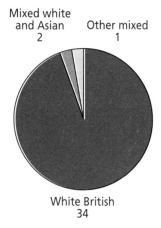

Number of children in affluent areas

RELIGION

Of all the adults interviewed, 56 per cent were Christians, 20 per cent Muslim, 2 per cent Buddhist and 22 per cent had no religion. Religious identity was related to ethnic identity and also tended to be more uniform in affluent areas. Those of white ethnicities were mainly Christian, a large minority had no religion, one white Turkish man was Muslim (the only Muslim living in the affluent areas) and one white British was a recent convert to Buddhism. All Bangladeshi adults were Muslim. Of the black African immigrants, two were Christian (from Uganda and Nigeria) and two were Muslim (from Ethiopia and Somalia). Of those identifying themselves as black Caribbean, three were Christian and two had no religion.

CURRENT MARITAL STATUS

In 27 per cent of the households, the caregivers were married or living together, 6 per cent of caregivers were in relationships but not living with their partner, 6 per cent were married but living separately, 19 per cent were divorced (and living alone) and 39 per cent were single. There were three families where the marital status given by the caregivers was not the same. This included one household where the main caregiver and partner started to live separately between the interviews with the caregiver and the partner, one household where a grandmother was co-parenting with her son and a household where the main caregiver and partner appeared to be cohabiting (and had five children together) but, while the main caregiver described herself as living permanently with her partner, her partner described himself as temporarily living with family.

There was a difference in the pattern of marital status between affluent and deprived areas. Most of the families in affluent areas were headed by single or divorced main caregivers (mainly mothers but including two fathers), while in deprived areas the two largest groups were those who were married or living together and those who were single. While lone-parent households made up 66 per cent of the households in the sample overall, they comprised 79 per cent of households in affluent areas but only 50 per cent of households in deprived areas.

The difference in pattern of marital status between affluent and deprived areas is probably related to differences in patterns of marital status between different ethnic groups. In deprived areas the large group of caregivers married or living together were mostly Bangladeshi and the majority of Bangladeshi households were headed by a married couple, while in the lone-parent household group the caregivers were mainly white or black.

HOUSEHOLD SIZE AND COMPOSITION

The average number of children (under 17 years) in the household was 2.5, ranging from one to five children and the distribution was very similar for both deprived and affluent areas. There were 14 single-child families, 23 with two children, 22 with three children and 11 families with four or five children.

Almost all families comprised a single adult or couple with children of one or both adults and very few had other relatives living in the household. Three couples had grandparents (their parents) living in the same household and there was one household where a grandmother was co-parenting with her son. Four families had older children (aged 17 to 20 years) still living with them.

HOUSING

The majority (83 per cent) of families were renting from the council or a housing association, almost the same proportions in both deprived (84 per cent) and affluent (82 per cent) areas. Just six families lived in houses they owned themselves (four from affluent areas and two from deprived areas). Three families were renting privately (two from affluent areas), one family from a deprived area was living in bed and breakfast accommodation and two families (one from each area) were living with relatives without paying rent.

EDUCATION

Of those parents who had gone through the UK school system (excluding those who had emigrated to the UK as adults), those living in affluent areas were more likely to have completed their schooling to the age of 16 (72 per cent compared with 42 per cent of parents from deprived areas). Over a third (37 per cent) of parents from deprived areas had dropped out of school by the age of 15 (two parents by 14). While roughly a third of parents from both deprived and affluent areas had attained O level or GCSE Grades A–C or equivalent, only two parents from deprived areas had attained anything above this level, whereas 25 per cent of parents from affluent areas had A levels (or equivalent) and 11 per cent had a diploma or degree.

There was little difference between ethnic groups in terms of educational attainment except that immigrants tended to show a wider range. While a large proportion (42 per cent) of the immigrant Bangladeshis had no qualifications, as did the one non-immigrant Bangladeshi, a third of immigrant Bangladeshis had attained A level or degree/diploma level in Bangladesh. Similarly immigrants from other areas encompassed the full range of qualifications, from none up to degree/diploma level.

It is possible that parents from affluent areas had better educational opportunities than non-immigrant parents from deprived areas (who therefore went through the same education system), while immigrant parents seem to have had much more varied educational opportunities. It also seems likely that immigrant parents face greater barriers to work, which might help to explain the presence of more highly educated immigrant parents in this sample.

Although the disparity between the number of women and men in the sample made comparisons difficult, there was an indication that the women in our sample of low-income families had achieved a higher educational attainment than the men. Eleven per cent of women had degrees or diplomas while none of the men did and a larger proportion of men had no qualifications at all (46 per cent of men compared with only 33 per cent of women). Many of the women with diplomas or degrees were lone parents and, in deprived areas, most were immigrants for whom English was their second language; these women therefore faced significant barriers to work despite their high educational attainment. At the time of the research, five women (but no men) were part-time students.

Although we sought a diverse sample, as stated at the beginning of this chapter, this description illustrates just how many sources of diversity there were. Parents living in poverty are a heterogeneous group in many ways. The next chapter explores both common issues and the relevance of a range of sources of diversity to their experience of living in poverty.

NOTES

1. Social services departments, schools and voluntary organisations used a range of methods to select those who might fit the parameters of the study to send the recruitment material to. Since families self-selected, we checked basic details of their circumstances while arranging interviews.

2. Caregivers included biological, adoptive and step-parents and also resident partners of parents (typically male partners of mothers) if they had been living in the household for two years or more.

3 Families living on a low inco — commonalities and diversities

Parents in our sample volunteered to participate in the research on the basis of their own self-definition of living on a low income. Most were wholly dependent on state benefits and, of these, only four had incomes above the poverty threshold,[1] all as a result of receiving disability and/or caring-related benefits (which compensate for extra costs or earnings foregone). Of the 19 households with an adult in some paid work, there were another four with incomes above the poverty threshold, one because they also received disability living allowance, and the rest because they combined paid work with benefits or tax credits and also had small families (one or two children). Those above the poverty threshold without the extra costs of disability to cover (three households) had incomes of £60 per week more at most. We have included them in the sample as their lives were more similar than different from those beneath the accepted threshold. All had been on incomes below the threshold in the past, and all clearly still worried a good deal about money. While crossing that line contributes to government targets, it may not of course be the point at which a difference is much noticed by the household concerned.

In this chapter we discuss first issues that crosscut the whole sample – what poverty meant in terms of their lifestyles, the restrictions it imposed and their ways of coping, their options and decisions regarding employment, and their experience of other sources of income (benefits, tax credits, debt and housing benefit). Much of this is familiar from previous research. The chapter then goes on to explore the impacts of diversity – of community context, and gender, ethnicity and class – on their experience. The material and social dimensions of poverty are interwoven throughout, but recognising the social dimensions (how people are perceived and treated by others) makes issues of diversity increasingly significant to understanding the experience of poverty.

THE EXPERIENCE OF POVERTY – COMMON ISSUES

We used a checklist of eight items and asked parents to check off those that they could not afford (see Figure 3.1). These were all very basic items, which the vast majority of the population would regard as necessities and which people would be unlikely to choose to do without. Eleven per cent of the sample could afford none of them, over a quarter could not afford a cooked main meal each day for each adult, and nearly half could not afford basic toys and sports gear for children or a day trip once a year. Ninety per cent of the sample could not afford a family holiday.

Figure 3.1: Parents saying they could not afford the listed items

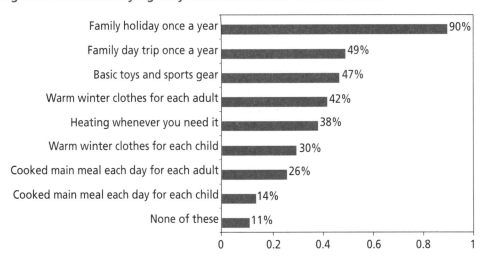

For most families, their budget was spent entirely on basic essentials, there was never any spare money and not enough at times to manage without borrowing. Where there was little if any scope for discretion, as found in other research, women were generally responsible for managing the budget (with the exception of Bangladeshi families, where men were more likely to manage money). Women were also more likely to say they could not afford all the items listed above (except the family holiday) than men. Forty-eight per cent of women said they could not afford warm winter clothes for each adult compared to 13 per cent of men. Thirty per cent of women said they could not afford a cooked main meal each day for each adult compared to 7 per cent of men.[2] 'Going without' is a common way of coping with poverty, which women clearly do significantly more than men (see also Lister, 2004; Pantazis and Ruspini, 2006).

Making ends meet took considerable time and organisation. Most women budgeted carefully, knowing exactly how much they had and how much things cost from where, and planning accordingly. Buying as cheaply as possible could mean travelling some distance or shopping around (though this was not always possible with small children). Using meters, key cards and fixed payment schemes for utilities could help to avoid debt, as could saving a bit each week towards bills or careful timing of their payment. Swapping clothes with friends as children grew helped, as did buying cheap and filling food, and cooking from scratch rather than using ready-made meals or takeaways. Constant juggling and prioritising was required despite such strategies. Examples of what many referred to as 'robbing Peter to pay Paul' included buying less food or missing a weekly bill payment if children needed new clothes or shoes, cutting back on food to pay for the repair of a bicycle puncture and alternating which child to buy something for each week. Very basic items become luxuries in this context – one woman talked of saving up to buy moisturiser, another of cigarettes as the only item she bought for herself. Others referred more generally to 'the little things that make you realise you ain't got what everyone else has got'. Breaking the law sometimes seemed a risk worth taking – one admitted to occasional shoplifting, another had been convicted of credit card fraud, a third person had thought about prostitution.

Poverty was often self-perpetuating. Life was sometimes more expensive than it needed to be – having no fridge or cooker, for example, meant buying food in small amounts or ready-made. Housing often had inefficient heating systems and poor insulation, which increased bills. Having no car could restrict options for work that might increase income. Health, energy and well-being were affected by poor diet (including inability to afford to meet special dietary needs, either for parent or child) and lack of labour-saving equipment. One woman without a washing machine did all her washing by hand, but it hurt her shoulders and the difficulty of getting all the soap out aggravated the children's eczema. Another had had to send her children to school smelling of urine after bed-wetting incidents, as there was insufficient hot water for them all to wash in the morning. Ordinary activities could consume more time and energy than usual, such as making a phone call when the phone had been cut off, and having to take children along to the local phone box and keep them occupied. Ill-health, disability or caring responsibilities meant some kept a car or took taxis when they could not really afford it, and had to cut costs elsewhere or go into debt to do so.

Being on a low income also undermined people's ability to live up to their own aspirations as parents, leaving them often feeling guilty and inadequate, whatever the circumstances that had led to poverty. Most were aware of the disadvantages conferred on their children by not having healthy diets and new clothes (or the right clothes), and not participating in similar activities to others (school trips, sports, leisure activities such as going to the cinema), but simply could not afford them. Even going to the park could cost too much when the expectation of an ice cream was included. Shared activities with children tended to be largely household shopping trips, watching TV or making things and colouring at home.

EMPLOYMENT

Paid work has consistently been advocated by the current government as the preferred route out of poverty and central to social inclusion. Many households are lifted out of poverty when an adult moves into paid work, and they may also benefit in other ways if, for example, the person's confidence, self-esteem and social networks are enhanced by the transition. Paid work does not always increase income, however (Bailey, 2006). Whether it does so depends on the availability and pay of local jobs, the education, skills and training of the person, the costs of childcare associated with working and the lost income from benefits or passported entitlements. Where employment does increase income, it may still not do so sufficiently to raise the household above the poverty threshold. That nearly half of children in poverty (48 per cent) now live in families where someone is in employment (Harker, 2006) is ample evidence that paid work is no automatic solution to poverty. Nor is it an automatic solution to social exclusion, since it may interfere with the time needed to maintain social networks as well as (for parents) with time for children (Gordon *et al.*, 2006, Chapter 5). Where a transition to paid work is made, it is also often not sustained – in a recent evaluation of the New Deal for Lone Parents, 29 per cent of those entering work from it had returned to benefits within a year (Evans *et al.*, 2005, cited in Harker, 2006). While many measures have been introduced recently to help parents (especially lone parents) to reconcile paid work with their family commitments,[3] some parents benefit more than others from these and there are still many barriers to entering, sustaining and progressing within paid work alongside caring for children (Harker, 2006).

The majority of households in our sample had no working members – 63 per cent in the affluent areas and 78 per cent in deprived areas were entirely dependent on benefits. Of those who worked, most worked part time, either just three to five hours per week, which allowed them to earn an extra £20 on top of benefits, or 16 to 20 hours, which qualified them for working tax credit (Figure 3.2). All of those working were in low-paid jobs (on or close to minimum wage) except for one woman in an affluent area who worked 16 hours a week as an administrator for a charity. One of the full-time workers in the affluent areas was self-employed but currently drew no salary from his business as the income was only sufficient to service the business loans.

Figure 3.2: Parents' work patterns in affluent and deprived areas

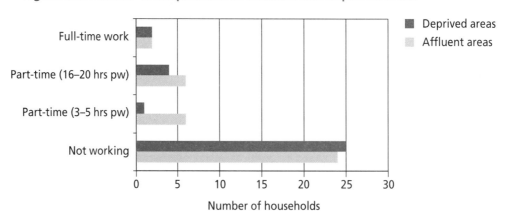

Several of those who worked enough to come off income support were worse off financially for doing so (after the loss of housing benefit, council tax benefit and free school meals, travel costs and the unpaid element of any childcare costs), but worked for the benefits to self-esteem and identity, or as a haven/escape from the rest of their lives.

Many wanted to work more than they did but had decided it was 'not worth it' (a recurring phrase) on the basis of such cost/benefit calculations combined with the likely effect of working on their relationships with the children, and had deferred plans until their children were older. Families claiming working tax credit are automatically excluded from free school meals and uniform grants, while those in receipt of income support or child tax credits with incomes below £14,155 are eligible. All but one of the nine families in our study who were claiming working tax credit, however (both in full-time and in part-time work), also had an annual income below this level. Their average incomes were £11,267 and equivalised incomes (taking family size into account) £10,263.

Constraints on the ability to take up paid work (or to work beyond a few hours) included all those already mentioned – the costs and availability of childcare, the structure of the benefit system (and its inflexibility – see below), lack of skills (including language skills) or experience, lack of jobs at sufficient pay to make it worth it, as well as immigration status (not allowing work), personal or partner's health (including agoraphobia, mental health problems, diabetes and other physical health or disability issues) and concerns about children. Since the childcare element of working tax credit can only be used to pay registered childcare providers, family and friends who offer to help cannot be paid for doing so, which made it harder for some to find suitable, affordable childcare. Health problems made an impact via the inability to manage working environments without excessive stress, the needs of a partner for care and the demands of hospital appointments. Concerns about children included the desire to care for those with ongoing special needs (e.g. autism) or in temporary distress (e.g. when a parent had left), or simply to 'be there' where a child was thought too young to tell the parent if something was wrong in substitute care or the parent was afraid children would get in with 'the wrong crowd' and get into trouble if they were not around.

Men and women were affected similarly by these constraints in many ways, but men who were unable to work expressed more sense of failure, guilt and weakness for not fulfilling a provider role than women, although some perceived it more as a positive choice where they had taken on a primary carer role after a partner had left or become ill. One of the latter had found his boss very unsympathetic when he had tried to combine work with childcare responsibility and felt that a woman might have received more support. Women's work histories are often argued now to be a matter of lifestyle choice, reflecting different preferences and priorities in relation to home and family vs. work (Hakim, 2000) – such choices as were made by our sample appeared far more influenced by constraints than by preference however. A few expressed a desire to 'be there' full time for their children as their priority, but many of these could not afford to do so and took on some part-time work. Many others would have preferred to be working, or to work more than they were able, but had to put caring responsibilities first (for partners as well as children) for lack of alternative options, either temporarily or long-term. Where caring responsibilities were likely to reduce over time, several were studying or training, or planning to retrain to work in future.

CASE STUDIES

Alison Conway is a mother of five children, aged three to 15 years, and has been almost entirely dependent on benefits since the birth of her first child. She has tried working but felt that it simply wasn't worth it, that she was only very slightly better off financially and too exhausted to give her kids the level of care they needed:

When I did work I had four children ... and I used to give ... half my wage for babysitting kids, cos I used to get up at six and come back for about half past six, and it were just knackering, it were just really knackering ... and it were just like £10 better off and I thought is it worth it? I haven't even got time for kids coming in, they haven't seen me all day and I'm like 'No, please, just leave me' so I had to jack it in. They don't make it easy for you.

Simon Ashworth is a lone father of two children, eight and ten years. Before his wife left them, he had worked all his life in various low-paid jobs: *'I've always paid my way, I've worked hard, I've paid my way, I've, you know, always tried to do the right thing and be honest'*. Before their separation, he was working shift work in a warehouse while his wife worked shift work in a nursing home – opposite shifts so they could share childcare between them, but this meant they rarely saw each other and, despite their long hours, they were still struggling financially: *'we were both working all these hours and looking after the kids and trying to do the house up and get bits and pieces, but we never sort of had money for holidays or going out'*.

When Simon's wife left and he became a lone parent, he tried hard to combine work with childcare but felt it was too hard on the children: *'I was doing six till two, you know, at work, drop the kids off at five in the morning and working till ten at night on the other shift, you know'*. He asked his employer if he could change his hours or have a different role *'I was prepared to work on any other job'*, but his employers refused and asked for his resignation *'[It] was understandable but I just thought they were a bit hard-nosed about it, I'd been there for over four years'*. When Simon applied for benefits, his decision to resign in order to care for his children was frowned upon and he was made to feel *'like [a] scrounger or benefits cheat'* despite his many years of working and the circumstances that had led to this difficult decision: *'I was embarrassed and ashamed anyway'* and he felt that, had he been a lone mother suddenly forced to give up work when her partner had left, the agency might have been more sympathetic.

Sarah Milton is a lone mother of two boys, five and three years. She was working in a care home before her first son was born and tried to return to work afterwards. She was working night shifts while her partner stayed with their son but was then having to look after her son during the day while he was out and was getting very little sleep, so she gave up and has been benefit dependent since. Her partner left before the birth of their second son and she doesn't feel it is worth trying to work while the children are still so young. Her oldest son is at school from 9.00 a.m. until 3.00 p.m., her youngest is at playgroup some mornings from 9.00 a.m. until 11.30 a.m., then she has to collect him and bring him home for lunch, then take him to nursery for 12.40, collecting him at 3.30 p.m. after her other son. With no qualifications, her only employment opportunities are low paid and after childcare she would not be much better off, while having less time and energy for her children. She has hopes of working in the future and has done some courses in basic English and maths through Job Centre training schemes, but doesn't feel it is a realistic proposition until both her children are in school full time and perhaps until they are old enough not to need childcare.

OTHER SOURCES OF INCOME

Other sources of income for the families in our sample included benefits, tax credits, and loans resulting in debt, each discussed below, and also ex-partners, children, families of origin (parents and siblings), friends, a pension (for one), savings (for one, without any entitlement to financial support as a result of immigration status) and grants from charitable trusts and voluntary organisations. By and large, people welcomed contributions from ex-partners where they were forthcoming, though often they were not, or the Child Support Agency's involvement meant the resident parent received little if any benefit. For one woman, her ex-partner's insistence on buying things only for his child and not for her (e.g. a family television that he insisted belonged to his seven-year-old daughter and did not have to be shared with her mum, and living-room flooring of his daughter's choice and against the mother's preference) made such support a rather mixed blessing.

Financial contributions or loans from other informal sources could be a lifeline, especially when benefit payments were delayed or in other crises, but also had to be managed in terms of their impact on relationships, and were sometimes a source of embarrassment or guilt. Grants from charitable trusts and voluntary organisations had also been a lifeline for some, covering essential items such as cookers, washing machines, school uniforms, shoes and other school costs, and facilitating opportunities such as a family holiday, a college course and training for parents with an autistic child.

Figure 3.3 shows the range of benefits and tax credits that families in our sample reported receiving. Almost a third (31 per cent) claimed benefits linked to illness or disability, reflecting the high level of such issues in the sample (significant barriers to work, as discussed above). In 21 per cent of households, one or more adults claimed either incapacity benefit or disability living allowance (two households claimed both); a further 10 per cent of households claimed disability living allowance for a child with disabilities (Figure 3.3).

Figure 3.3: Benefits claimed by parents in sample

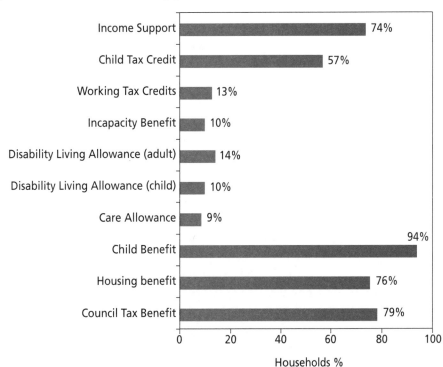

Households %

Overall, 13 per cent of households were receiving working tax credits (Figure 3.3). One of the families where an adult was working full time did not claim tax credits; this family's situation had changed recently when a working partner had moved in with a lone mother and child previously dependent on benefits. They had stopped claiming means-tested benefits and now were entirely dependent on his (low) wage and the mother had not realised prior to the interview that they might be eligible for working tax credits.

Dealing with the benefits system

The benefits system is a vital source of income, but could also be a significant source of stress and uncertainty. A few families reported no problems with it, and positive aspects mentioned included the value of passported benefits, free prescriptions, direct payments into a bank account, and independence of income after leaving an abusive relationship, as well as support to study or retrain accessed through the Job Centre. Social fund grants and loans had also been a big help to those who received them, and had been used to buy a range of essential items, including fridge, cooker, washing machine, flooring, furniture, bed linen, clothes, as well as to decorate, pay off debts and subsidise Christmas and holidays. Some official exclusions had been circumvented with the help of advice workers, e.g. buying school uniforms (not allowed) by claiming for children's clothes (allowed).

Many families continued to find the system a real struggle to negotiate, however. Problems with claiming included finding information about entitlements difficult to access and understand, the advice received was sometimes confusing, and forms and letters were complicated. Written information was particularly hard for those without fluent English, but it was a white British man who complained most forcefully about endless forms, which he found too complicated to fill in correctly and which got sent back repeatedly, leaving him feeling they were a way of avoiding payment (*'forms, upon forms, upon forms'*).

Late payments, often unexplained, left some without enough money for food and/or forced to go into debt. Payments that were temporarily stopped altogether when circumstances changed and a reassessment had to be made, and requests for repayments, were similarly extremely hard to manage for those whose finances were very finely balanced. Disputes over entitlements, for example when the rate paid for disability living allowance (DLA) was reduced and the parent appealed, were stressful. Several also complained of being made to feel small and of feeling degraded or disrespected in their interactions with benefits offices, and had expected greater sympathy and understanding over such issues as unexplained late payments. Courtesy, sensitivity and a responsive and efficient service are entirely reasonable expectations in exercising what are citizenship rights, expectations that are reinforced by frequent reference to claimants and other users of public services as 'customers' now.

Some similar problems had been experienced with housing benefits and council tax benefit. One parent had had their housing benefit (HB) stopped after they failed to reply to a letter requesting more information about two adult children – the letter had been delivered to the wrong address (as was apparently common in that block of flats), but the parent was £1,600 in arrears by the time this was sorted out. Another failed to declare her child tax credit when claiming for council tax benefit, an oversight amidst a messy divorce and depression, and as a result she both lost her council tax benefit and got a warning for fraudulent claiming.

Tax credits   The introduction of working tax credit to supplement the incomes of those in low-paid work and subsidise childcare costs was hugely helpful to many of the families in our sample, and was described by one parent as 'the best thing that ever could happen, for me'. Again, however, there were a number of problems (which apply to both working tax credit and child tax credit), which made the system stressful to engage with – including the difficulty of working out how much people were entitled to, long waits for payments (despite repeated chasing), which pushed some into debt, disputes over overpayments and underpayments and demands for large sums in repayment, and slow responses to changed circumstances. This all creates considerable uncertainty, and the complete stopping of payments when overpayment was detected until the amount was recovered, could cause unmanageable fluctuations in income. Some of these problems are now being addressed, but the impact of reforms, especially to the system for recovering overpayments, will need to be kept under review. In addition, the loss of passported benefits attached to income support, and the inflexibility of the system in responding to complicated circumstances, could be significant barriers to take-up of paid work. One parent had been advised by the Job Centre not to take a job as a school cook, as the system would be unable to cope quickly enough with the change from her working in term (entitled to working tax credit) and not working in the holidays (needing to claim income support).

Debts   The majority of the families in our sample had some debt, as do the majority of the population probably – the British were recently reported to have a higher average level of debt than any other European country (Datamonitor, 2006). If comparison is made to owner-occupiers' mortgages, the extent of the debts may not be particularly high. However, the kinds of debt and the relative extent (and consequent repayments) proportional to disposable income are more distinctive to low-income families. As well as bank overdrafts, credit and store cards, kinds of debt included rent, council tax and utility bill arrears, overpayments of tax credit, catalogues, social fund loans, loans from family, friends and children, and high-interest doorstep loans. Although a few families had avoided debt or paid just 3–5 per cent of their weekly income in debt repayments, most paid 10–35 per cent of their weekly income and at least 11 per cent were paying 60–70 per cent of their weekly income in debt repayments.

Attitudes to debt ranged from a determination to avoid it where possible to positive acceptance that it could help, with many in between resigned to it as the 'only way to cope'. Many distinguished between different types of debt and did their best to avoid doorstep loans. Reasons for going into debt included covering the cost of basic essentials such as clothes and shoes for children, utility bills, furniture, washing machines, carpets, as well as for some items that may appear less basic – a large TV, Sky, birthday and Christmas presents, a car, a holiday, to have friends round – but are part of everyday life for most. Several had gone into debt when benefits or tax credits were held up or stopped for some reason. Unexpected costs, as a result of damage done to property, burglary or fire, or when a period in hospital interrupted earnings, pushed others into debt. One went into debt to sustain a drug habit and another during a psychotic episode when her spending had been influenced by delusions. Some were in debt as a result of the mistakes of others (usually the council, the benefits agency or the tax office), or the malicious actions or irresponsibility of others (usually ex-partners).

The impacts of debt can be many. Most obviously, the costs of repayments cut into already limited budgets, sometimes to the extent that going into further debt is the only way to manage everyday expenses. Fear and worry about what action may be taken (debt collectors or bailiffs appearing, requirements to attend court cases, bankruptcy, utility disconnection, eviction or repossession) can create huge stress and uncertainty. The loss of control as the 'vicious cycle' of debt mounted and people lost track of what was owed to whom or what needed to be done to avoid charges being increased, and the prospects of escaping debt receded, left some overwhelmed, with a sense of failure and despair, and they were coping largely by denial. Family relationships were affected by these emotional impacts, which were evident in the distress with which some people talked about debt in the interviews. They could also be affected by people's attempts to hide what debt they'd accrued from their partners (or other family members), by different attitudes to debt that created conflict and by a partner working long hours to pay off debts without any benefit to living standards.

Some had succeeded in paying off debts, had renegotiated a more manageable repayment plan (often with help and sometimes involving a consolidation loan, which could make life simpler but also more expensive in interest), or had found a way to make debt work for them (setting themselves strict limits, developing a system for paying off one debt at a time so they had a good record of paying back and could borrow again while they paid off another, and/or keeping detailed records of each transaction). Managing to get out of debt altogether was a significant achievement.

Sources of advice and help

Many families found vital advice and support in managing benefit and tax credit claims and debts (as well as a range of other issues, especially housing problems) from Citizens' Advice Bureaux (CABs) or other advice agencies. Workers explained people's entitlements, made phone calls for them or told them what to say when they made them, helped them fill in forms, supported them in appeals or meetings with, for example, a housing officer, applied for grants or loans and offered help with budgeting, all of which was extremely valuable help. Several parents had got a support worker to negotiate with services or debt collection agencies on their behalf because they felt the worker would both be better able to present their case and be taken more seriously, whereas they would be dismissed as trying to get more than their due or escaping their responsibilities. For parents managing very much alone, workers could also become a source of personal support, 'someone there' for them, beyond the practical support offered. A few had had negative experiences of such agencies, either where a worker was inexperienced or did not seem to understand them (more common for those with limited English), or where the time involved in accessing help felt excessive, with long waits to see an adviser or they had to chase up to get action taken.

THE EMOTIONAL AND PSYCHOLOGICAL IMPACTS

Parents we interviewed talked of the emotional impacts of poverty in terms of lack of choice and opportunity to make changes (feeling trapped or 'in a box'), of a sense of guilt and failure (particularly in relation to their children, discussed more in the next chapter) and of high levels of uncertainty (over health, income and expenditure) making it difficult or simply too stressful to plan ahead. A lone parent, who worked part time, had three children aged five to 11 and felt like she never stopped, put the latter impact very clearly. She worried about debts and not having a pension, and was being helped by a housing support worker to develop a five-year plan, but said in practice she had trouble planning five hours in advance. The unpredictability of life on benefits, whereby changed circumstances, mistakes or disputes can lead to sudden changes in income, and the insecurity of much of the available paid work for those who also have childcare responsibilities, contribute significantly to this kind of difficulty.

The time involved in managing life on a low income, often in response to unexpected events, was a striking theme. As one said:

> *But this is the thing, it's hard, what do you do first, you know. We're just trying to get through stuff every day and then you've got … to do this, to do the whole housing thing is just… oh that's a full-time job in itself, and I've not really had the energy to do it. But now I think we will, we will start pursuing that a bit more. Because we can't stay like this.*

SOURCES OF DIVERSITY

Parents living in poverty are by no means a homogeneous group. While there are many commonalities in the experiences described above, there are also many ways in which their experiences vary. The next sections discuss the influence of community context and socio-cultural context. Chapter 4 addresses the influence of biography or life history.

COMMUNITY CONTEXT

There is a widespread belief, with some evidence to support it (Atkinson and Kintrea, 2001; Fitzpatrick, 2004), that it is worse to be poor in a poor area than in one that is more socially mixed. Much recent policy has been focused on the concentration of disadvantage found in highly deprived neighbourhoods, e.g. via area-based initiatives such as Sure Start. Poverty in such areas is often combined with high crime rates, high unemployment, poor amenities and conditions, and restricted opportunities, affecting health, well-being and satisfaction with life, and low aspirations are easily passed on from generation to generation. Those who are poor in a more mixed area, however, may face a different set of issues related to greater local inequality, which have been relatively unexplored. Our data suggests, as did a previous qualitative study of the views of practitioners in both deprived and more affluent contexts (Atkinson and Kintrea, 2004), that each kind of community context may disadvantage families in poverty in rather different ways, although there were also many similarities across community contexts.

Housing

Families we interviewed in the deprived areas had some truly appalling housing conditions (including cold, damp, draughts, leaks, dangerous gas and electricity systems, cockroaches and overcrowding), which could clearly impact on children's health (see Chapter 5) and be demanding for parents in terms of pushing unresponsive local authorities to tackle them (see Chapter 6). While some similar problems existed in the 'affluent context' sample, in terms of overcrowding and poor housing conditions, they were less evident and less extreme. Some different housing problems occurred in the affluent context, such as a lack of affordable housing and the expense of heating a large house.

The associations of a particular house were a source of stress for some in both contexts. Where the house remained the family home after a relationship breakdown, it could be a reminder of that loss. In two cases, housing also carried painful associations with abusive parents – in one case because the house was owned by the father's parents and he had no means of leaving it, and in another where a room had been decorated for the mother by her father who had sexually abused her in childhood.

Heating was also sometimes made unnecessarily expensive in both areas, by poor insulation, ill-fitting windows, ineffective systems and/or slow repairs. Overcrowding in both areas could be intensified by the needs for extra space of a particular child (e.g.

a room of his own for an autistic child or one with behaviour problems 'to have paddies in') but could also contribute to behaviour problems, with children of different ages living in each other's pockets. One lone parent with six children, the oldest of whom was 17, living in a three-bedroom house with all the bedrooms tiny in a deprived area, described it as 'like living in a sardine can'. Unsuitable housing in poor condition, and/or temporary housing that could remain a home for as long as five years, were huge sources of stress for families, especially in the deprived areas.

Neighbourhood context

There were also greater fears about crime (including gun crime), drugs, racism and unsafe neighbourhoods in the deprived areas, with associated fears for both parents and children's safety, and many parents anxious about their children being influenced by or drawn into drugs or anti-social behaviour. Some kept their children inside, despite lack of space, to avoid them getting into trouble. Families in deprived contexts were more likely to feel negatively about where they lived than those in affluent contexts, to a large extent because of the impact of local street culture on their children. Previous research has found parents' attempts to influence children's behaviour (through monitoring and/or punishment) less effective in deprived areas (CSCI, 2006, p. 31), suggesting that their fears are well founded. Some women also avoided going out themselves for fear of being attacked.

Families in affluent contexts usually had safer environments for themselves and their children, although some lived on estates with a relatively poor reputation within that location. They generally had safer space for children to play outside, although the children sometimes had fewer others to play with, whether because of being on different income levels from neighbours, lack of children of a similar age in the neighbourhood or living at a distance from children's schoolfriends. Although relatively little crime was seen as a benefit of the neighbourhood in affluent areas, there were often specific threats identified (e.g. a known 'paedophile', a violent ex-partner, or a particular group of lads or 'bad family') and some similar fears and strategies in relation to children.

In both contexts, some parents felt safer than others, and being familiar with the neighbourhood, being known and knowing others, played a significant role in such feelings. Both conflicts and good relationships with neighbours occurred in both contexts. Several families in the deprived areas, however, talked of a lack of cultural integration between different BME groups – this tended to be viewed positively by insiders to the group concerned (giving a sense of belonging) and negatively by outsiders (contributing to isolation).

Access to amenities and services

Families in the deprived areas tended to have better access to affordable (or free) amenities and facilities for children, to live close to schools, shops, mosques, churches and community centres, and to have better transport links than did families in more affluent contexts, although even relatively low costs, combined with the effort involved, could inhibit use of facilities, as could the condition of those facilities or their other users. For those in the affluent areas, affordable activities for children, cheap shops and many services were at a greater distance and less easily accessed (without a car), and there was simply less available tailored to the needs of low-income families. Services such as counselling and childcare were provided primarily by the private sector. Some were lucky enough to have a nice park or playground nearby, and such free facilities were generally in good condition and relatively safe, but the awareness of many facilities out of reach (for whatever reason, cost, time and/or transport) was a significant source of frustration and stress.

The professionals we interviewed also commented that low-income families were often reluctant to use what facilities there were, e.g. mother and toddler groups or even swimming pools, in affluent areas, because they felt they would stick out as noticeably different in predominantly middle-class environments. Children in deprived areas were twice as likely to go swimming or to regular sports sessions (e.g. karate, football training) than children in affluent areas (57 per cent compared with 23 per cent), partly because free or cheap facilities were more available and partly because the lack of safe places to play outside meant some parents made extra efforts to make this possible. More children also attended after-school clubs in deprived areas.

Poverty, inequality and social exclusion

In both contexts, parents were aware of the pressures on children to keep up with their friends by having the latest toys and the 'right' clothes and trainers, but parents in the affluent contexts had higher standards for their children to live up to. They worried about their children being unable to have, for example, similar kinds of (expensive) birthday parties, leisure activities (e.g. horse riding) and foreign holidays.

Children in the affluent contexts also had a much clearer sense of their families being on a lower income than their friends than did those in deprived contexts, although children in both contexts were mostly aware of material lack. When shown five money bags of increasing size and asked to indicate where they would place their family's income level and then that of their friends' families, children in affluent areas consistently chose the smallest money bags for their own family and a larger money bag for their friends' families, typically two money bags larger. Children in deprived areas picked all sizes of money bags for their own family's income and were just as likely to choose smaller as larger money bags for their friends' families. The children's perception of their own family's relative poverty within their local context was quite accurate and children as young as five years old showed this awareness. Children in deprived areas were just as likely to feel sad about not having things or experiences, however, and to wish for more money, more space at home or material things for themselves or their families. Children in both contexts also had a wider range of concerns, for themselves (including better family relationships and more friends), for their families and sometimes for the world or particular groups (poor people in other countries, for example). Children in the deprived contexts were more likely to wish for an end to violence and crime.

Professionals commented that children from low-income families were more likely to stand out as different at school in affluent areas, often had an internalised sense of difference too and could have a tough time as a result. Low-income families could easily become perceived as a problem or the source of other problems in schools where they formed a very small minority, and where schools were less familiar with their situations. An example was cited by health visitors of a poor family in a primarily middle-class school who had clearly been scapegoated, both by other parents and teachers: '*they're almost picked on by the teachers I think cos they don't fit into the middle-class standard and they're almost ostracised by other people and also scapegoated. If anything goes wrong it's all blamed on that one family*', although the health visitors saw the family as coping well. Schools were also focused primarily on a middle-class market and, without the specific resources allocated to deprived areas (see Chapter 6), may give relatively little attention to the needs of low-income children. While schools in deprived areas tend to be disadvantaged overall (HM Treasury/DfES, 2005, p. 34), the disadvantages faced by poor children in more affluent areas may be obscured where comparisons are based on school averages.

The differences should not be overstated. Even in areas of high deprivation, inequality is often highly visible, both in schools and in the wider environment, and there is considerable variation within as well as between both deprived and affluent areas. The situation of low-income families in affluent contexts merits more attention, however. While in some contexts lower demand on services may mean needs are better met, in others families may be disadvantaged by lack of accessible services or feel more 'under the microscope', both from professionals and other service users. Professionals who wished to develop services tailored to low-income families had often been frustrated in the affluent contexts by lack of funding, political will or community support, and the combination of lack of familiarity and frustration may easily result in more blaming or 'othering' of poor parents for their own situations. At the same time, professionals working in highly deprived areas talked of the risk of overfamiliarity with poverty, and of becoming immune and not noticing it any more, and may sometimes fail to give due recognition to the challenges it poses as a result.

SOCIO-CULTURAL CONTEXTS – GENDER, ETHNICITY AND CLASS

Gender, ethnicity and class were also important aspects of the context of family members' lives, interacting in many and complex ways to influence identities, experience and opportunities. Sixty-seven women were interviewed (all main caregivers, including 44 lone parents) and 15 men (four of whom were main caregivers, two lone parents). Both partners of a couple were interviewed in 12 households. In the deprived areas, the sample was very ethnically diverse, with the largest group being Bangladeshi families, followed by white British, then smaller groups of black Caribbean and black African, and a few of other white, Asian and mixed ethnicities. In the affluent areas, 95 per cent of the sample were white British, with the remainder other white.

Although identifying themselves with a class position was not straightforward for many parents, in both areas there was a small number of families who had clearly 'fallen into' poverty from a more comfortable middle-class lifestyle. In the deprived areas, all but one were Bangladeshi families who had been well off in Bangladesh. In the affluent areas, they were white middle-class families whose income had dropped as a result of divorce, ill-health or bankruptcy. Some ways in which the interviewees' diverse social positions affected their lives and experience have been discussed already (in relation to gender and ethnicity), and others will be mentioned later in the report. Here we discuss some key issues for appreciating the nature and extent of diversity.

Consistent with other research, women in our sample were more constrained by childcare responsibilities from paid work than men but had somewhat less of their identities invested in it, although the priority they accorded paid work varied. Some felt guilty about working (and being less available to their children), others, especially those from middle-class backgrounds, about not working (and therefore failing to conform to their own standards as a good role model and provider for their children). Bangladeshi women were less likely to consider working outside the home, for both cultural and language reasons, but one, a lone parent from an affluent background, was studying and planned to work.

Women also tended to take more responsibility for the management of money (except in Bangladeshi families) and to spend on other members of their families before themselves. Some also experienced restrictions rather differently from most men, being more likely either to accept 'going without' as what women do (sometimes across generations of their family) or to find some satisfaction in ensuring their children were provided for. Men seemed to feel restrictions on spending more keenly, partly because of gendered expectations of demonstrating status by buying for others outside the family (a round of drinks for mates for British men, gifts or food for family gatherings for Bangladeshi men), although also because their expectations of personal money were higher. Where we were able to interview both partners in a two-parent household, women, however, reported higher levels of stress than their male partners.

Parents from middle-class backgrounds were less experienced at managing on a low income and often distressed by the loss of their former status as well as the lack in their everyday lives. For some, a sense of personal failure and shame was acute, especially where they maintained contact with former social networks. In the case of white families, friends and family evidently retained a much greater range of options than they now had. In the case of Bangladeshi families, relatives in Bangladesh still expected a financial contribution and/or visits from them based on their location in an affluent country. For some women who had left a violent partner, however, the autonomy more than compensated for the loss of income, and having someone else clearly to blame mitigated any sense of personal failure.

The aspirations of formerly middle-class parents were often higher for their children than those of parents for whom poverty had been a long-term state, sometimes over generations. Damaged self-esteem and a sense of difference could be a barrier to their own and their children's relationships with other local families, however, and to their use of local resources. Parents for whom poverty was a long-term state were more likely to have friends and family in a similar position living close by. However, since they too were on low incomes, they were not always able to help out financially. By contrast, for one Bangladeshi women parenting alone, her main sources of social support were all overseas, though she was in frequent contact by telephone. Although there was a Bangladeshi community locally who she found friendly, most came from a poor and/or rural background. Their differences made it difficult for them to understand each other and mutual support occurred infrequently.

Overseas telephone calls, visits abroad, sending money to family members back home (which one family still managed to do occasionally) and classes in Arabic or Islam for children could all add significantly to the expenditure of Bangladeshi families, but some prioritised them in order to maintain both social networks and cultural traditions that were important to their identities. Safety and/or earning capacity had been undermined by racist abuse, threats or discrimination in the local community and/or at work for some Bangladeshi, other black and white non-British parents and also for one white parent with mixed-race children. In this context, the preference some expressed for living in an area where the population was predominantly from their own ethnic group was unsurprising.

While the relationship between religion and ethnic identity was not straightforward, all the Bangladeshi adults we interviewed were Muslim, though religious practices were more important to some than others. A traditional sexual division of labour – with men assuming the financial provider role and authority (unless delegated) and women having responsibility for children – was common but also sometimes resisted. One Bangladeshi man clearly found pressure to be the provider from the extended family as well as from his wife stressful. One woman who had left a violent partner talked of Bangladeshi women's need for empowerment through education: '*I was you know very shy … don't want to go anywhere or … talk with other people … but* [after doing courses] *I can talk when I go to shop or with GP … it gives me courage that now I can*'. Another Muslim woman (from Somalia), also a lone parent, spoke positively of the freedom from traditional dress and oppressive control of women and girls that she and her children enjoyed in the UK. A mixed-race (white and Asian) British woman whose ex-partner had been a strict Muslim also described a form of domestic violence in which he had attempted to impose traditional values, authority and dress on her, and had belittled her for failing to meet his standards.

STIGMA
– A COMPLEX AND
MULTIDIMENSIONAL
ISSUE

The experience of stigma – of feeling one's identity spoiled or discredited – may contribute significantly to low self-esteem, and also to social isolation, as people attempt to control and manage information about potentially stigmatising circumstances within their social interactions. There were many sources of stigma evident in our interviewees' accounts, although what was stigmatising in one context might not be in another, and people managed the threat of stigma in different ways, some achieving a sense of pride in overcoming adversity or brushing off negative reactions more easily than others.

Aspects of poverty that some in our study found stigmatising included being excluded from the range of options open to others (including to buy new clothes or the right new clothes, to participate in similar activities and to exchange hospitality or gifts), being dependent on benefits (and having to attend the benefits office or identify oneself as entitled to free prescriptions at the chemist), being in debt and not working (increasingly for women as well as for men). Stigma can also be attached to particular deprived neighbourhoods, both where these are fairly extensive and where they are small pockets within a more affluent area, although it was perhaps experienced most keenly by individuals in our study who felt they stood out as poor in an affluent context – one reported feeling watched by security staff in shops as 'the single mum likely to steal'. Those in deprived contexts reported many similar sources of stigma to those in affluent contexts but some also referred to the comfort of knowing others in similar situations.

Histories of domestic violence or childhood abuse, estrangement from families of origin, being a lone parent, mental health problems, investigation for child protection concerns, criminal convictions and contact with professionals over parenting difficulties or children's behaviour problems (discussed in later chapters) could all attract stigma too, often affected by gender, ethnicity and/or class in some way. Among BME (especially Bangladeshi) women, the stigma attached to domestic violence, to mental health problems and to poverty were all particularly intense. The impact of stigma on the ability to access services is discussed further in Chapter 6.

> **WHAT SOME PARENTS SAID ABOUT EXPERIENCES OF STIGMA**
>
> *Well when people, I suppose really it's people know that I'm on my own a one-parent family, they obviously know that I'm going to be on a low income. So that does affect, especially when a lot of them are, you know, they're married and they don't know what it's like, they don't have a clue at all, they almost like look a little bit down at you ... you do get put in a certain class.* (Lone mother, affluent area)
>
> *Yeah for definite. I was at bus stop other day, I was talking to this lady, she was very friendly and all rest of it, and she said something 'Where does your husband work?' I said 'I don't have one'. I said 'I'm a single parent' and that was it. 'Oh benefit scroungers' and all this, I thought if only you knew love ... She actually come out with it. I walked off, I thought I either walk off or I have a go, and she were only this little old lady so I walked off, I went to a different bus stop.* (Lone mother, affluent area)
>
> *You begin to feel like you're a scrounger, a low life, a good for nothing, you're permanently on benefit. Nobody can see that I spent a lot of time in the Forces, that's why my legs, my knees, my hip's knackered, nobody can see that.* (Father, unable to work for health reasons, affluent area)
>
> *I feel people look at us differently to other friends/family – they feel sorry for us and say not to buy presents or bring food for social gatherings or family events. Their pity makes me feel low. At times we avoid these situations. Other members of the family wear better clothes than me – they make me look like I wear cheap clothes and saris.* (Bangladeshi woman, deprived area)

NOTES

1. We used equivalised incomes (adjusted for household size) and the commonly used definition of 60 per cent median income before housing costs for these calculations. The information is not wholly reliable, however, given the sensitivity of questions about income, the different definitions that parents used (e.g. before or after tax credits or loan repayments) and the uncertainty of some about their exact income.

2. While these statistics are based on different-sized samples, 66 women and 15 men, the difference was in fact greater on some items (e.g. ability to afford warm winter clothes for adults) where we were able to interview men and women in the same household.

3. These include: the extension of maternity and paternity leave and pay; increased availability of, entitlement to and financial support for childcare; the development of out-of-school childcare; increased rights to unpaid leave for family commitments and to request flexible working; and increased subsidies for those in low-paid work through tax credits.

4 Parenting through adversity – interwoven stresses and supports

KEY POINTS

- There were very high levels of stress among parents in our sample, reflecting the impact of poverty and associated issues such as poor and/or overcrowded housing, and also of the high frequency in our sample of other forms of adversity, including childhood maltreatment, domestic violence, relationship breakdown, bereavement and mental health problems. The challenges of parenting in poverty were affected by complex interactions between the parents' biography or life history and their current social circumstances. Some life experiences made poverty more difficult to manage and poverty made all other forms of adversity more difficult to cope with.

- Parenting was an important source of identity, self-worth and satisfaction for most. An absence of other socially valued roles or sense of identity and self-worth could make it difficult to seek or accept help with parenting difficulties.

- Both unresolved past abuse and ongoing abuse (from ex-partners or parents) left some parents struggling to exercise control and authority over their lives in terms of partnerships, parenting and managing on a low income. Some women who became parents as a result of rape had particularly difficult relationships with their children.

- Contact with ex-partners and disputes over contact with children were a significant source of stress for lone parents, though a few ex-partners offered regular and reliable support and/or childcare.

- Children with behaviour problems posed particular challenges (especially in overcrowded conditions). Mothers with histories of childhood abuse and/or domestic violence sometimes felt further victimised by children who were aggressive and violent to them and their other children, and found such behaviour extremely difficult to manage. They were more likely to engage with professionals over these issues if professionals acknowledged their own experience as well as their children's.

- Support networks were affected by poverty and constraints on time, but also by histories of childhood maltreatment, domestic violence, relationship breakdown, immigration, levels of stress and gender. Men had fewer supportive friends than women and tended to rely heavily on partners.

- Different sources of support offered different kinds of support. Parents who had supportive relationships with their own parents had a quality and extent of support not available to others, although friends played a different and important role.

The extent of stress among our sample was very high compared to other research with parents in poverty. Fifty-one per cent of our sample scored 8+ on the Malaise Inventory (where 7+ is associated with a high risk of clinical depression), compared to 21 per cent in Ghate and Hazel's sample. Scores of 8+ would be expected in 7–7.5 per cent of the general population (Cheung and Buchanan, 1997, cited in Ghate and Hazel, 2002).[1] Only a few parents were not struggling in terms of their own well-being, leaving aside their children's for now. This reflects our sampling strategy, which, by including many families in contact with social services, reached more troubled families than are often reached by research, alongside those managing their lives with some satisfaction despite poverty.

The life history approach we took allows us to explore how the challenges parents faced could reflect, not only the experience of living in poverty that we described in the last chapter, but also the accumulation of disadvantage over a lifetime and many other interwoven stresses. In this chapter, we place participants' experience of parenting in biographical context, discussing their own childhoods, their partner relationships and routes into parenthood, their changing relationships with partners and the challenges of parenting particular children or in particular contexts. While many of the issues covered are familiar 'risk factors' (e.g. parents' own childhood experiences of abuse, domestic violence, large families), a view from the outside, focusing on multiple problems, assessment and risk, can obscure the reality of lifelong and ongoing struggles with many forms of adversity, and the pervasive impact of poverty on them. We then discuss parents' social networks and the impact of their life histories and current circumstances on them, since social support is known to be important in buffering the impacts of stress.

PARENTS' EXPERIENCES OF CHILDHOOD AND FAMILIES OF ORIGIN

Parents we interviewed had had a wide range of childhood experiences. Some had grown up in relative affluence, others in poverty. Some described happy childhoods, with close and loving family relationships creating security, and support always there for them to buffer the impacts of adversity. Others had experienced more conflict and stress within their families, and had little support to cope with the impacts of poverty and deprived neighbourhoods, or experiences such as separation and loss, or family members affected by physical or mental illness. Many (over 30 parents) described maltreatment, from their parents, other family members or other (mostly known) people outside the family. It is likely that more people had experienced maltreatment than spoke of it. Some could remember little about their childhoods and amnesia is a common impact of childhood trauma. Others gave conflicted accounts, which suggested the image of a 'happy childhood' they held on to protected them from a more mixed and painful reality. Some took the opportunity that the interview offered to speak of these experiences for the first time, others chose not to talk about their childhoods.

MALTREATMENT AND OTHER FORMS OF CHILDHOOD ADVERSITY

Experiences of maltreatment or other trauma included sexual abuse (mostly by fathers, father figures or brothers), physical abuse (including violence from siblings, as well as, for some, harsh and persistent beatings by parents), emotional abuse (also by siblings as well as parents) and neglect, exposure to domestic violence against mothers, witnessing of atrocities in the community (for those who had grown up in countries with political or civil violence) and forced marriage (at the age of 13 for one). The majority had experienced more than one form of abuse. Some experiences, which might not in all circumstances be traumatic, had been so – one man felt effectively abandoned by his parents at seven when they left him in Bangladesh with relatives and came to the UK to build a new life, and the sense of loss still haunted him. The fear, or terror, which accompanied such experiences created insecurity, often compounded by a range of other experiences of instability or loss. These included bereavement, the loss of a parent or parent figure when family relationships broke down or new partner relationships proved transient, when a parent moved abroad or foster placements ended, and changes of residence due to living in temporary accommodation, refuges or residential care.

Some parents in the study had carried excessive responsibility from an early age, either to care for a parent suffering from ill health, bereavement, alcoholism or domestic violence (which sometimes involved missing school for fear of leaving their mother with a violent partner), or to protect siblings from an abusive parent or substitute for an absent one in looking after them, and sometimes to look after both parent and siblings. This early sense of responsibility could be intensified by their own abuse, with the guilt and self-blame often attached to it, and/or neglect, where children were effectively abandoned or left to fend for themselves. While these are common impacts of abuse, they may have their roots in experiences with very specific and personal meanings. One woman who grew up witnessing severe domestic violence from her alcoholic father to her mother, and who was sexually abused by an older brother from the ages of four to 12, then spent a year in residential care. When she returned to the family home, her brother expressed his remorse for the pain he had caused her by regularly self-harming in front of her. In turn, she felt guilty and responsible for his behaviour and eventually turned to alcoholism for escape.

Abuse had affected other relationships than that in which it occurred, both within and outside the family. Domestic violence could terrorise and control all members of the family. Abuse by a parent or sibling often left the person experiencing it angry with the other parent for not protecting them, whatever their capacity to do so might have been. Fear and shame could inhibit people from telling other family members of abuse, and some were uncertain about whether others had known, a sense of betrayal corrupting those relationships. For some, other family members, including extended family, had definitely known and done nothing (whether because they were too afraid of the perpetrator themselves, as had clearly been the case in one family, or because of conflicting loyalties, fear of the consequences of reporting or other reasons), undermining trust in them and in adults in general. Friendships were affected for some by feelings of inferiority and difference, and some interviewees had been bullied as children in response to physical neglect (and some had truanted from school or left early in response). Abuse was often kept hidden, and only seven participants had contact with outside agencies in relation to their abuse in childhood. Five had contact with social services, but four of these described it as unhelpful and ineffective for a range of reasons, largely a lack of sufficient attention to their own experience and needs. One had also contacted the police several times over her stepfather's violence to her mother, but again, when help had arrived, it had been short-lived and ineffective.

IMPACTS ON ADULT LIFE

For many of our interviewees, then, managing stressful and traumatic experiences began at an early age and their expectations of others, including agencies, were low with good reason. For some, the impacts of maltreatment or poor experiences of care and family relationships were relatively resolved as they approached adulthood. For others, conflicts continued and the effects rippled onwards and outwards through their lives, affecting their relationships with partners, their parenting and their social networks (see later sections), as well as their own well-being and mental health.

In the sample as a whole, 58 parents self-defined as having suffered from a mental health problem at some point in their life (most commonly depression, ongoing for many, but also anxiety, agoraphobia, bi-polar/personality disorder, obsessive compulsive disorder (OCD) and schizophrenia). Twenty-three of these parents described experiences of childhood maltreatment. The remainder had gone through a range of experiences of care in childhood, with the majority at the more negative end. That childhood maltreatment increases the risk of a range of negative outcomes, including mental health problems, drug and alcohol problems, revictimisation (especially for women), offending and parenting problems, is clear from other research, although there is no inevitability about such impacts and many factors mediate. Negative outcomes are more likely where abuse is severe, long-lasting, takes multiple forms or involves multiple perpetrators, occurs both in childhood and adult life and/or is recent (see Hooper, 2003 for review).

A range of experiences other than childhood maltreatment, both in childhood and later, were also identified by our participants as contributing to mental health problems, including domestic violence, rape, relationship breakdown, bereavement, ongoing family conflicts, poverty-related stress and parenting problems. The potential impact of all these on mental health is also recognised in other research, although it is more common for mental health problems to be seen as increasing the risk of parenting problems than the other way round.

Factors that may protect against negative outcomes, which have been identified by previous research, include supportive relationships with an adult or siblings in childhood, good school experiences or other activities that lead to positive recognition, strong social support networks, therapeutic intervention and supportive non-abusive relationships in adult life (professional or informal) (Hooper, 2003). In this study, only three parents who had suffered maltreatment in childhood did not go on to experience either domestic violence or mental health problems. Two of these had come to the UK to build a new life, one at the age of 25 seeking refuge from community violence in Somalia, the other at 19 for employment opportunities. The woman from Somalia saw the abuse she had experienced from her parents as part of the cultural norms of her country of origin. Although it is not clear whether that perspective had come before or after migration, the distance that migration had given her from that part of her life and the perception of abuse as a collective rather than an individual experience (and hence with less privacy, secrecy or self-blame attached to it) may have been protective, although the experience had clearly been traumatic. The third had escaped her abusive family young, and soon after met a partner with whom she still had a happy and supportive relationship. Other participants described a range of factors that had helped them come to terms with histories of abuse or to manage their impacts – including support from family (especially siblings, with whom childhood experience could sometimes be shared and reflected on), friends and professionals, education, employment and training (which could offer structure and routine as well as self-worth and identity), participation in voluntary work or community or religious activity (also a source of self-worth and identity as well as, sometimes, social support), belief and the role of religious faith.

While many had achieved some degree of resolution of the past, for some, conflicts (including ongoing financial and emotional abuse) continued with families of origin. It is increasingly recognised that separating from an abusive partner does not necessarily put a stop to abuse, and the same is true of abusive parents and siblings. Both unresolved past abuse and ongoing abuse (which may of course be interrelated in a range of ways) could leave parents still struggling to exercise control and authority over their lives in terms of partnering, parenting and managing on a low income.

PARTNERING AND BECOMING A PARENT

We interviewed many more mothers than fathers. Those fathers we interviewed were a particular subset of those we heard about – largely those who had lived with their children from birth, although a couple had left and returned to the same family, and a few had joined families as stepfather to older children and were now father to the youngest. Probably largely because of the sample (the result of availability), most of the fathers interviewed had had children with partners (often wives) who they were in committed relationships with. The majority remained with them, although there were two lone fathers who had become the primary caregiver after separating from their wives. The context within and process by which the women we interviewed had become mothers was more variable however, and this had an influence on how they felt about their child or children. Some had deliberately planned to become mothers, others had had unplanned pregnancies as a result of sexual risk-taking, and four had become pregnant through rape.

Deliberate motherhood occurred in two different ways. For some, it was part of a traditional life plan, involving forming a stable partnership or marriage first and having children within that. For another group, it was a kind of 'ticket out' of a troubled childhood and adolescence (a way of leaving the family home, gaining an adult identity as a mother, and creating a relationship to give and receive love and affection within). This route tended to be taken quite young, often in the mother's teens. While most hoped to parent with a committed partner, a few appeared to have little expectation of such a long-term commitment (possibly due to their own poor experiences of care from fathers) and to have viewed parenthood as something they set out on very much alone. One woman who suffered multiple forms of abuse by her stepfather moved to London at the age of 16 and said of this time in her life:

> *I really wanted a baby ... I would have slept with anyone to get pregnant. Because I wanted at that time my own family, you know, you speak to a lot of people who have gone through the same as what I've been through and all they want is a family to love. That's what I wanted ... I love my sons to pieces but it didn't all work out the fairytale I wanted it to.*

That a history of child sexual abuse (Rainey *et al.*, 1995) as well as of being looked after by local authorities – itself also often the consequence of maltreatment (Knight *et al.*, 2006) – are associated with an increased risk of teenage pregnancy (alongside other influences including social deprivation, low aspirations and lack of employment opportunities) is well established by research, but often overlooked in policy.

Unplanned pregnancies had occurred in a range of contexts – including one-night stands, brief relationships, occasional sex with friends and long-term relationships, sometimes after having other children. Those who had them had had mixed responses. Some had found pregnancy frightening and traumatic, and two had denied and hidden it, one because she was 15 and scared of the consequences (her mother only found out when she went into labour), the other because she had been recently bereaved and was too overwhelmed to cope with the idea of motherhood then. For others, the decision to continue with the pregnancy was difficult, either because of an uncertain relationship with the father or because of the costs and demands of another child. One woman who had had sex with a friend with whom she did not otherwise have a sexual relationship then decided to have the baby, believing (rightly) that he would be a better co-parent (albeit non-resident) than the fathers of her three previous children, all of whom had been abusive. A few felt 'saved' from lives of high risk and little purpose (often involving drugs, alcohol and/or petty crime) by such a pregnancy and the responsibility, respectability and identity that motherhood offered.

For the four women who became pregnant through rape, in two cases the rape took place after many years of abuse by parents (in one case by a fellow resident in supported housing, in the other by her mother's partner). In the third case a woman who had just arrived in the UK from Uganda (with no previous experience of abuse) had been first gang-raped then raped a few days later by her uncle – she did not know who had fathered the child. In the fourth, a woman who was forced into marriage at 13 was terrorised and effectively raped by her husband – he also allowed other militants in the village to make threats of rape to further intimidate and frighten her. In all these cases, their first and sometimes only child was conceived in this way. In the first three cases, the mothers had mixed feelings about these children, being reminded by them of the rape itself, the perpetrator and associated experiences of abuse. They were conscious that anger they felt towards their children was sometimes derived from these associations.

Becoming a parent, a mother or a father, offers people a new social identity, one with diverse, changing and sometimes contradictory social meanings. What it means to particular individuals may reflect aspects of their biography (particularly their own experiences in childhood), their current options and the various routes they have taken into parenthood, as well as contemporary cultural discourses (Hollway and Jefferson, 2000). Identities and their meanings are revised and renegotiated over life as people move in and out of different contexts and roles, although where they are serving a defensive function, such adaptation may be resisted. By and large our participants, when asked to describe the characteristics of a 'good mum' and a 'good dad', tended to do so in fairly similar ways (in terms of love, care, support, guidance, time and involvement in children's lives). At the same time, the majority of fathers interviewed subscribed to a fairly traditional model of fatherhood in which they were head of the family and responsible for providing and protecting. These traditional values were often presented as a cultural norm but were essentially very similar across British, Bangladeshi and other households.

In practice, parenting was still a clearly gendered role, in terms of both identity and activity, although the two dimensions were not always in line. While fatherhood was an important identity for all the men we interviewed, their active involvement in parenting ranged from those who were the sole or main caregiver (as lone parents or when their partner was ill or disabled), through the majority who contributed significantly or shared parenting with their partner, to those whose parenting role seemed almost non-existent, a potential playmate for children but not effectively a parent. Some fathers took considerable responsibility for parenting tasks, an active father role seeming to offer a substitute identity to a provider one and considerable pride and satisfaction. Others maintained a traditional head of household role and identity, despite unemployment, by continuing to delegate all parenting and domestic tasks to their wives. Others seemed genuinely confused about what their role should be and lacked confidence in how to 'do' fatherhood. In these circumstances, some fathers (both biological and stepfathers) removed themselves from demanding situations, leaving them to their partner to deal with. This was sometimes because they saw mothers as more central (especially where the father was semi-resident) and their own role as peripheral, sometimes because they did not know how to communicate with children, set boundaries or exercise authority themselves. While, in most of the families where both biological parents were still resident, the partner relationship was a key source of support for both mother and father, in families with a father in 'adult child' role, the mother had extra demands, emotionally and financially, from her partner, with little if any support. There was less variability in the roles that mothers took with children, reflecting the more tightly prescribed social expectations of motherhood. For both mothers and fathers, the reality of parenting was often different from their expectations, however, and the inability to live up to their own ideals was a significant source of stress. This inability was often because of the restrictions that poverty imposed, but could also be triggered by changing circumstances (especially partner relationships and new challenges from children's behaviour).

STABILITY AND CHANGE IN PARTNER RELATIONSHIPS

Stable partnerships could be an important source of support for parents as well as a significant relationship for children. Partnerships were also a site of violence to many mothers (as well as sometimes to their children – see Chapter 7 regarding risks to children). Thirty-two (51 per cent) of the women we interviewed (but none of the men) had experienced domestic violence in adult relationships. Nineteen of these had also experienced childhood maltreatment and 17 of these were now parenting on their own, a few with ongoing conflict with both families of origin and ex-partners but most estranged from them. While some explained their partnering with violent men in terms of their childhood experience, largely via the impact of low expectations – or, as Herman (1992) puts it, the acceptance of violence as 'the inevitable price of relationship' – others who had not experienced childhood maltreatment also experienced violent partnerships, and their ex-partners too often continued to be emotionally abusive, controlling and threatening. For some women, the domestic violence had started during pregnancy. Domestic violence occurs across all income bands and the high incidence in this sample is probably partly because we sampled intentionally to include families with maltreatment issues (and domestic violence is a known risk factor) and partly because many of those we interviewed were lone parents who had escaped domestic violence (and for whom poverty was the result).

Changing relationships with partners were the context in which many became a parent or a different kind of parent – a lone parent, non-resident parent or step-parent – although all of these statuses could be or become long-term and stable.

LONE PARENTHOOD Some lone parents had effectively always been lone parents, for others it was the result of relationship breakdown, in many cases as a result (at least partly) of domestic violence. Those who became lone parents after relationship breakdown often had less household income than before. Where the partnership had involved financial abuse, they sometimes felt (and were, in terms of access to income they could spend on the household, children or themselves) better off, but some lacked confidence in their ability to manage money or work in the aftermath of such a relationship. Parenting alone was one of their main sources of stress, but other stresses included the ongoing contact with abusive ex-partners and managing their children's contact with non-resident fathers (abusive or not – see below). For those with no such contact, there was often ongoing fear – some mothers and children remained in hiding and afraid of an ex-partner even after a few years without contact. This may have been partly the impacts of trauma (via post-traumatic stress disorder) but could also be realistic fear. In one case, an ex-partner had recently moved back to the area and resumed a previous campaign of intimidation. In another (Bangladeshi), a separated husband had tried to follow a child home from school to find out the family's current address.

Abusive relationships had often severely undermined women's confidence in their parenting during the partnership, and for some they continued to do so after separation, sometimes in direct contact, sometimes via the child and sometimes both. One non-resident father who was a strict Muslim continued to criticise the child's mother (who was not) to their son during contact visits, telling him she was a bad person and would go to hell for her lack of religious belief. When they met, he constantly belittled the mother telling her she had nothing to offer their child. She was left both undermined herself and dealing with a child who was insecure in his relationships and confused about how to behave in terms of Islamic practice.

For some lone parents, particularly those who had had to be self-reliant from an early age, managing on their own was viewed as a personal strength and achievement. It undoubtedly was, but the defensive investment in such self-reliance could also make it difficult for them to access or accept help when needed. In some lone-parent families, one child, usually the oldest, sometimes took on a more adult role in the household, becoming a confidant to the mother, having responsibility for and authority over younger siblings, and helping with household or family decisions. While the boundary between appropriate and inappropriate responsibility for children is a debatable one (which varies in different social and cultural contexts), the well-being and development of children who took on such an adultified role, with the emotional responsibility it entailed, could clearly be affected. One nine-year-old girl regularly stayed up late for 'girly evenings' with her mother, which both enjoyed, but she found it hard to get up in time for school in the mornings. A mother who described her eldest son aged 17 as 'like a husband' (in terms of being a confidant) also found it difficult when he behaved like one, trying to control the time she spent with her new boyfriend.

NON-RESIDENT PARENTHOOD Non-resident parenthood (mostly fathers but including three mothers in our sample) was described mostly from the perspective of the resident parent (the mother), though four of the fathers we interviewed also had children from previous relationships living elsewhere. Of those four, only one had some (very minimal) contact with their child. In most of these cases the lack of contact was due either to conflict during the breakdown of their relationship with the mother or uncertainty over paternity. The one father with occasional contact was allowed it only if he contributed financially, which he was rarely able to do, being dependent on benefits and having two children from his current relationship to support. Non-resident parents were described mostly in negative terms, unsurprisingly given that most separations had involved considerable conflict, many fathers had been violent to their partner and/or their children while resident, and conflict and abuse had often continued after separation. Some of these fathers now had no contact with their children because of concerns for the children's safety and well-being. Some fathers had made their own decision to sever contact, either immediately or over time, sometimes as they became involved with new families, sometimes believing that a 'clean break' was better for their children. A couple of fathers had disappeared at the news of pregnancy and had never met their children.

Other non-resident fathers did have ongoing contact with children, and in a few cases this was regular and reliable, or sometimes limited but still supportive. In these cases, conflict between the parents was largely resolved and parents were able to communicate with mutual respect over their children, still sharing that interest and supporting each other. One woman, whose husband was bedridden because of ill-health and required 24-hour care, had three children from different relationships and good relationships with all of the fathers, although one lived in Jamaica. The two local fathers were important figures in the children's lives, looking after their children most weekends, providing vital respite for their mother. They also contributed financially and were involved in making parenting decisions:

> *Sometimes I've got both of my ex-husbands here and everyone's like 'this isn't normal'.*
> *It's normal for me. And my kids are lucky, fortunate, they've got three dads, like wow,*
> *you know.*

In between these two groups was a group of non-resident fathers with some contact and involvement, but where ongoing conflict and unreliability made it another source of stress for the resident parent (and their children – see next chapter). Many of these made little financial contribution. Mothers in these cases found it extremely demanding trying to negotiate the balance between maintaining their children's relationships with their fathers (which were often important to them) on the one hand and protecting the children from the risks that contact entailed (including exposure to drug use and culture, as well as abuse) on the other. Having to explain broken promises to children, sometimes frequently, was also stressful. Some mothers had also experienced a great deal of pressure from professionals, particularly within the court system, to allow abusive fathers access even when the children did not want contact. The mothers' accounts of domestic violence and abuse had sometimes been treated with scepticism, and their children's clearly expressed preferences had sometimes been discounted (see Chapter 5 for further discussion).

STEPFATHERING   Few stepfathers were interviewed, though some fathers were both biological and stepfathers to children. Some of the accounts of stepfathering also come from mothers' perspectives. New partners who became stepfathers could be an important source of support for the mother, and some had developed warm and loving relationships with their stepchildren, becoming a source of support for them too. Others offered little financial contribution to the household, mainly because they themselves were dependent on benefits and had a very limited parenting role. Some mothers seemed to prefer new partners to have such a limited role, keeping control of parenting themselves and limiting their children's attachment to a parent figure who might not stay around. For some this in part reflected the impact of past experiences of abuse, domestic violence or previous partner relationships on their ability and willingness to trust men.

The effects of the cohabitation rule on entitlement to benefits were also a source of stress and instability. One stepfather had been working full time (on a low wage) before moving in with a new family. The fact that his partner lost her benefits and became wholly dependent on his income was hugely stressful for them both. He was pushed into poverty by it and found it difficult to adjust his spending habits, finding it hard not to be able to buy a round of drinks or even a sandwich with his mates at work, and often spending money without realising that his partner had earmarked it in their account for bills. Conflicts over money, combined with a stepdaughter's behaviour problems and pressure from the mother's ex-partner, led them eventually to separate. They had continued to have a relationship, now had a child together and were planning to live together again as soon as he found full-time work. He felt he now understood the financial commitment and had come to accept the restrictions this would involve.

THE CHALLENGES OF PARENTING IN POVERTY

The restrictions and demands imposed by living on a low income were described in the last chapter, as were the feelings of guilt and inadequacy that people described at not being able to afford things they knew would leave their children disadvantaged in relation to their peers. Most of the parents in our study were, however, dealing with numerous other traumas and difficulties, including histories of or ongoing abuse (rape by boyfriends and others as well as childhood maltreatment and domestic violence), mental and physical ill-health, relationship breakdown and bereavement. Seven parents had lost children, either through miscarriage, stillbirth, cot death or (in one case) murder. The extent of such problems reflects both the nature of our sample and the higher incidence of both ill-health and child death among lower than higher socio-economic groups (Bradshaw, 2002; Bradshaw and Mayhew, 2005).

Unresolved trauma, ongoing conflict and abuse, mental health problems and the impacts of stigma on self-esteem could all seriously undermine parents' energy for developing the activities with children that contribute to mutually satisfying relationships and their capacity to adopt the authoritative style associated with optimal outcomes for children.[2] Authoritative parenting has been found to be positively associated with satisfaction with social support (Ruscio, 2001). Adverse life experiences and stigma may therefore undermine it to a large extent via their impact on support networks (see later in this chapter). In our study, parents who were more permissive in style were less able to manage the pressure to spend more than they could afford on children, feeling unable to say no to their children's requests or set appropriate boundaries to spending on them. As a result they seemed more likely to go into debt, compounding their difficulties. A permissive parenting style was also associated with more conflict with children over what they could have or do because parents failed to be consistent and children knew they might get what they wanted if they asked enough. Parents who were more authoritarian in style faced different stresses from poverty, as the many uncertainties accompanying it often undermined their control over their lives and any conflict with children could be a further threat to that control, to which they sometimes responded with violence.

Parents who were authoritative in both establishing boundaries around behaviour and managing a tight budget were more confident in their parenting and tended to have good relationships with their children. All parents derived satisfaction from the aspects of parenting they felt they did well, however (often simply being there for and talking with their children). Many were proud of managing to be good parents despite adversity, took pleasure in their children being happy or doing well (at school, in other activities or socially), and felt the rewards of parenting (especially children's love and affection) helped them to keep going in difficult circumstances. Even in the context of very difficult and conflictual parent–child relationships, parents treasured small expressions of affection from their children. The rewards of parenting tended to be scarcer and the stresses greater where children had special needs and/or behaviour problems, and in some large families.

CHILDREN WITH SPECIAL NEEDS OR BEHAVIOUR PROBLEMS

In the sample families, there were children with many different types of special need, including conditions described or labelled by parents as physical and mental health problems, non-specific physical and learning disabilities, autism, attention deficit hyperactivity disorder (ADHD), dyslexia and dyspraxia. There were also many children whose parents described them as having various behavioural problems, which were sometimes associated with diagnosed conditions (such as autism or ADHD) or had been labelled as such by professionals – for example, when a child had been statemented in school or been offered treatment with child and adolescent mental health services (CAMHS). The term behaviour problems was used fairly loosely, often for behaviour that was challenging but had no other clear label – by and large we follow parental definition in discussing it, though sometimes the children themselves or their siblings also spoke about problem behaviour.

Different special needs posed challenges for parents to varying extents and in different ways. Children with mental disabilities that meant their developmental stage was behind their chronological age were not necessarily any more challenging to parents than other children. In two families with such children, poverty and past traumas were far more significant sources of stress. Other disabilities or special needs could be more stressful, especially where parents lacked confidence in their ability to meet the child's needs or manage their behaviour. Autism was particularly challenging for parents, as children were less able to make friends and thus were more dependent on their parents for play, and ordinary tasks and explanations took longer, leaving parents with less time to meet other children's needs. Undiagnosed disability was also particularly stressful and worrying. One family, whose child had physical and learning disabilities, had little understanding of his condition, needs and prognosis, but both stayed at home full time to care for him. They rarely took him or their other two children out and felt unable to discipline him. The child was bored and frustrated with his restricted life. Health problems were a worry and could involve frequent and time-consuming medical appointments.

Behaviour problems ranged from very serious aggressive and violent behaviour (often entailing constant verbal and sometimes physical attacks on the parent and/or siblings, and sometimes involving peers), through behaviour that put the child themselves at risk (violent tantrums, running away or self-harm), to parent–child conflicts of varying regularity and intensity, which could be seen more as difficult parent–child relationships. Some parents linked their children's behaviour to experiences of family disruption, loss, trauma, abuse or previous lack of care for various reasons (including physical or mental health problems, drug use and domestic violence). Others believed it was inherent, describing the relevant child as difficult from birth, and some had more than one explanation. Parents often found such behaviour extremely difficult, feeling out of control and able only to endure rather than manage or cope with it. The difficulty of managing such behaviour was an additional constraint on activities outside the house and some parents felt trapped by it, keeping their children at home most of the time.

Some parent–child conflicts were poverty related – for example, where parents had to deny children things they wanted and this became a flashpoint for conflict, or where children used the parent's lack of money (and sometimes their own access to it from other family members) to humiliate the parent or challenge their authority. In such circumstances, the parent's feelings of inadequacy at their poverty were compounded. Having a child with behavioural problems also often made it more difficult for parents to manage on low incomes because of the costs incurred when children destroyed household items, siblings' possessions or damaged things belonging to other people. When behavioural problems were particularly severe, these were often cited by parents as a barrier to work because the child was regularly sent home from school and excluded by childcare providers so that the parent had to be home for that child.

Mothers with histories of childhood abuse and/or domestic violence experienced violence from their child (usually sons but in two cases daughters) as further victimisation, and indeed it did seem part response to trauma, part imitation of a violent father. Other parents, both men and women, with histories of childhood abuse also found conflict with children more difficult to deal with, as feelings associated with previous victimisation were restimulated. In some cases, fairly normal if challenging behaviour could become a problem partly because of such associations. In many families, both child and parent had a history of abuse, and any conflict carried echoes of those earlier experiences for both, easily contributing to their escalation. For some of these parents, becoming a parent had been a way of escaping a difficult childhood, and the combination of the impacts of their own maltreatment and the investment they had in parenting as a source of self-worth and identity (often feeling they had failed in other areas of life) made criticism of their parenting from children particularly difficult to bear. Such behaviour undermined the parent's ability to parent the child who was exhibiting the behaviour and often their other children as well.

Among parents and professionals there were a continuum of explanations, with parents tending towards the position attributing the problem to the child (either their inherent characteristics or their past experiences of trauma) and professionals tending towards the opposite position and attributing unmanageable behaviour problems to parents' failure to parent adequately. In reality, there are probably often complex interactions between these (and other) factors, and difficult situations evolve over time, sometimes escalating, sometimes getting effectively stuck, with a child sometimes continuing to 'act out' in response to a risk that is no longer there, or a parent continuing to scapegoat a child as 'the problem' in a more complex situation. Parents whose fragile self-esteem was based very much on their perceptions of themselves as good parents found professionals who immediately perceived all parent–child conflicts as due to their own parenting difficult to deal with, especially where their child was violent and aggressive towards them and they experienced it as abuse. Interventions were more likely to have been successful if professionals had acknowledged the child as an actor in the situation at least to some extent. In most of the severe cases, parents had eventually got such acknowledgement (via a statement or diagnosis of ADHD) but it had often taken some time and was usually accompanied by little successful intervention (see Chapter 7).

LARGE FAMILIES   Large families are defined here as those having four or more children. There were 11 large families in the sample, split almost equally between affluent and deprived areas, most with four to five children, but one with eight children (three of whom were now adults but still living at home). All large families experienced some degree of overcrowding, but, while those in affluent areas were all housed in at least three-bedroomed houses, some large families in deprived areas were housed in two-bed houses. While, in affluent areas, sleeping space (albeit crowded) was always found in bedrooms, in some large households in deprived areas, children were sleeping in living rooms. Typically, the parent or parents would have one bedroom and children of the same gender would share. This worked better when there were similar numbers of boys and girls in a family. When a five-child family consisted of four girls and a boy (or vice versa), the group of same-gendered siblings were usually crowded into one room despite large disparities in age, so that a young teenager might be sharing with a toddler. A few large families also had a child with behavioural problems and this made sharing of sleeping space particularly difficult for siblings. Overcrowding was one of the factors that contributed to sibling conflicts and increased parents' stress.

Having more children also made most parenting tasks more difficult and therefore more stressful. There were more children to organise and get out of the house in the morning, more meals to provide and washing to do, parents were more likely to be dropping children to more than one school (or more likely to let their secondary-aged children go alone because they had to stay with their primary-aged children). The demands were increased of course for lone parents, particularly those who were isolated and without any help – and five of the 11 large families were lone-parent households. More children also made participation in any activity that entailed a cost more expensive. Children from large families were much less likely to participate in sports courses or organised groups that had fees attached. Even when these fees were very modest, parents could not always afford to find even £1 for four or five children every week. It was also more expensive for large families to go anywhere that required paying for transport or where the children might expect a treat such as an ice cream at the park. Parents of large families often preferred not to go rather than have to deal with children's demands and disappointment. As a result, large families were often more housebound, particularly in deprived areas where there were few safe outside play areas in the neighbourhood. This also tended to contribute to conflict both between siblings and between parents and children.

So far in this chapter we have described the range of stresses involved for our participants in parenting. For some, poverty was clearly the major source of stress. For others, a different issue, especially poor or overcrowded housing, children's behaviour problems, ongoing abuse from ex-partners or families of origin, or unresolved traumas including child maltreatment or rape were the most stressful issue. For many, it was impossible to separate out what was most stressful about parenting on a low income – as one put it, '*everything is stressful*'.

The final section explores the nature of parents' social networks and the support (and sometimes further stress) they experienced within them.

INFORMAL SUPPORT NETWORKS

Parents' informal support networks appeared similar to but slightly more restricted than those described by Ghate and Hazel (2002) for families in their sample. While almost all parents (95 per cent) had at least one person they could count on in their informal support network, the mean number of people giving some form of support was five (compared to six found by Ghate and Hazel) and a smaller proportion had large informal social networks including more than ten individuals (9 per cent compared with 12 per cent found by Ghate and Hazel). The majority of informal support networks included some family (most often parents and siblings if present) and some (typically three) friends; resident partners were usually but not always included (17 per cent of parents did not include a resident partner as a source of support) and about a quarter of lone parents included ex-partners; 21 per cent included resident partner's family and 10 per cent ex-partner's family. There were no differences in size or composition of social networks between families living in deprived or affluent areas.

The nature of support given by different types of members of networks differed. When present, the parent's own parents contributed substantially more practical and financial support, as well as emotional support, than any other member. Grandparents often provided free childcare, and bought gifts or paid for activities for children and/or the family. Support of this kind provided by parents was obviously limited by the resources they had available. Interviewees who had dropped into poverty and whose parents lived on much higher incomes had potentially greater contributions than those from a background of long-term poverty whose parents were living on similarly low incomes. Similarly, some parents had more time to offer practical help than others. However, the extent, quality and impact of the support offered depended also on the nature of the relationship that parents had with their own parents, and this will be explored more fully below.

Just over half of parents included siblings in their support networks and a quarter included other family (aunts, uncles, cousins, grandparents and sometimes children). Siblings were often very important sources of emotional and moral support, sometimes practical support but rarely financial support. In some families, older siblings had had a partial caregiving role in the family when they were growing up and continued to have a relationship that had elements of a parent–child relationship with their younger sibling. Other family members were usually less significant sources of support except for a few interviewees where aunts, uncles, grandparents and even adult cousins had been their primary caregiver in childhood and therefore had more of a parental role in their lives. Some parents included their children as key sources of support and, while some were adult children, some were as young as eight years old. The kinds of support that parents received from their young children included practical help around the home and emotional support.

When a parent had a resident partner, they were usually the key source of emotional and practical support. Fathers with resident partners tended to rely almost solely on them for emotional support. Mothers with resident partners also usually cited partners as their primary source of emotional support, but more often had other friends or family who provided additional support. For some parents with no further contact with their own families of origin, their partner relationship also provided a link to a different extended family and support within that. The importance of supportive partner relationships was particularly strongly felt by those families with a disabled or autistic child, or where one parent was suffering from mental or physical ill-health. Those mothers who did not cite resident partners as part of their informal support network included some families where the partner took little responsibility in the home (both stepfathers and some biological fathers to the children) and some where the parents appeared simply not to confide in each other.

Non-resident ex-partners, when they gave any support, usually provided only limited financial and practical support focused on their children, buying clothes and other items for them and caring for them for limited periods. While resident parents acknowledged this contribution from non-resident parents as support because it helped them, they also recognised that the support was really aimed at the children and at giving the father access and a role in their child's life. When the relationship between the separated parents was difficult, the contribution of an ex-partner could be experienced both as supportive (e.g. because it might give a resident parent respite when children were away with the partner) and emotionally stressful. However, when the relationship between separated parents was good, ex-partners were often a key source of emotional and practical support (and sometimes financial if they had available resources, which was rare).

Friends were primarily a source of emotional and moral support, often the key source of this kind of support. Friends also provided some practical and occasionally financial support, but usually on a reciprocal basis. Friends often helped with childcare and sometimes helped with practical chores (e.g. shopping, decorating) and, although there was no formal arrangement for exchange, the parent would usually (although not always) be helping their friend in the same way, according to each other's need. Occasionally, parents were able to borrow small amounts of money from friends, which they would usually pay back very quickly; sometimes, the parent would also lend to the friend. Unlike financial support from parents and ex-partners, which tended to flow one way into the family, financial support from friends was more a temporary help with cash flow rather than an additional resource.

INFLUENCE OF ETHNICITY AND IMMIGRATION ON SUPPORT NETWORKS

Ghate and Hazel (2002) found that, contrary to the cultural stereotype of large extended families, minority ethnic parents actually had smaller informal networks than white families. However, in this study, there was no difference in the size of informal networks between British-born parents of white or minority ethnic identity. Parents who had immigrated to the UK as adults did have much smaller informal support networks, however, typically with less than three members as compared to over five members for parents who had been resident in the UK all their lives.

Parents who had immigrated to the UK as adults and had therefore left their family of origin behind were far less likely to include family in their informal network simply because they were not available. Just 13 per cent of these parents included their own parents in their networks (compared with 71 per cent of other parents) and just 53 per cent had any family at all in their networks (compared with 91 per cent of other parents). Of those who did include family, contact was usually limited to phone calls. For these few, overseas family were often a key source of emotional support but could not offer practical help and very rarely financial assistance. Parents who had immigrated to the UK as adults also had fewer friends than other parents (typically nought to two compared with three to four). Parents who had immigrated to the UK as children, travelling with or to join their parents, usually had social networks similar in size and nature to other parents.

INFLUENCE OF
CHILDHOOD
MALTREATMENT ON
SUPPORT NETWORKS

Of those parents who had living parents resident in the country and who had suffered childhood maltreatment or a very poor experience of care from their parents, two-thirds were estranged from their parents and did not include either parent in their support network. Where childhood abuse had been perpetrated by only one parent or by another family member (sibling, grandparent), parents usually still had contact with the non-abusive parent, or both of their parents if neither had been abusive. Sometimes they had become estranged from non-abusive parents because they felt those parents should have protected them from the abuse. Only a small proportion of those who were estranged from their parents had no family at all in their social network. Most maintained contact with siblings and sometimes other family members.

Some (16 per cent) of those who had experienced childhood maltreatment by their parents still included those parents in their social network. Most who did so had very mixed feelings about the support they received from this source. Parents often maintained the relationship because of the benefits they saw for their children both in terms of having a relationship with their grandparents and in terms of the material benefits that the parent could not otherwise provide. Benefits to themselves in terms of respite childcare (when often there was no other possible way of getting this) also played a role in the parent's decision to maintain the relationship. For these interviewees, the support received from their parents was also a source of stress and they often described it as limited to practical and financial support for their children but definitely not a source of emotional support for themselves.

The support these interviewees received from their parents could be quite substantial and often very similar in practical and financial terms to that provided in families where there had been no childhood maltreatment. It appeared superficially that these parents had very good levels of support from their parents but in fact the history of the relationship meant that it was often a key source of stress for parents. One woman had only recently cut off contact with her mother, having achieved the confidence to do this after several years of counselling. There may have been other parents too who would have preferred to stop contact with their parents but were unable to do so.

A few parents had a slightly different experience. A couple had undergone some kind of restorative process during childhood, one with support from social services involving temporary care and one with support from grandparents, which had enabled them to resolve their feelings and develop good relationships with their parents in adult life. A small number also downplayed the impact of their experiences of abuse on their adult sense of self and on their relationships with their parents, accepting it as a cultural norm (where physical abuse occurred in a disciplinary context), or describing it as not the whole of the relationship (where heavy beatings apparently occurred in the context of a relationship otherwise often loving and supportive) and/or as a traumatic experience from which they had learned and grown stronger. There may have been an element of denial in these accounts, but the meaning of abuse and hence at least part of its impact could also be influenced by context, in terms of both relationship and culture, and opportunities for restorative care could mitigate them.

INFLUENCE OF MENTAL
HEALTH PROBLEMS ON
SOCIAL NETWORKS

There was very little difference between the informal support networks of parents with either current or past mental health problems and those with no history of mental health problems, in terms of the average size of informal support networks and the numbers of family and supportive friends they had. Those with no history of mental health problems were slightly more likely to have a partner or ex-partner in their social network. They also had more interest-sharing friends (people they enjoyed being with but who did not offer support) – an average of four compared with an average of two for those with past or current mental health problems. However, for a few parents, all of Asian ethnicity, mental health problems (their own or a partner's) clearly had contributed to social isolation, as they felt excluded from their community by their perceptions of stigma, and had become very housebound as a result, having little contact with friends or family.

Parents with high malaise scores (i.e. high levels of stress) had fewer supportive friends than those with low malaise scores, however (an average of two compared with three), and correspondingly smaller support networks. Ghate and Hazel (2002) also found that parents with high malaise scores had smaller support networks and they proposed a link between current depression and reduced social support. However, in this study, we had both parents' malaise scores and their own reports of whether they were currently or had in the past suffered any depression or other mental health problems. We found that, while parents with higher malaise scores had smaller support networks, those who reported depression (past or current) did not. Since smaller support networks are associated with stress levels rather than mental health problems *per se*, it may be that smaller support networks contribute to stress, or that other factors both increase stress and restrict social networks.

RESTRICTIONS ON SOCIAL NETWORKS

A substantial number (44 per cent) of parents in our study did not include either of their own parents in their social networks, for reasons related mainly to childhood maltreatment and/or immigration (discussed above), although a few also had parents who had died. Only 17 per cent of parents had no family at all in their social networks, either having become estranged from their whole families because of childhood maltreatment or having lost contact after immigration.

Almost a third of parents had no friends in their support networks and another quarter had just one supportive friend. The factors that contributed to restrictions on friends in social networks varied widely. For a small number, childhood maltreatment had impacted on their self-esteem in such a way that they found it very difficult to establish close friendships. These parents often spoke of being self-reliant and of not wanting to discuss their problems with anyone, and frequently had friends with whom they shared interests but from whom they kept much of their personal circumstances hidden. However, most parents who had experienced childhood maltreatment had similar numbers and qualities of friendships to other parents.

Poverty was one of the most commonly cited barriers to forming and maintaining friendships. Most parents found it difficult to afford a few pounds for a drink or coffee or bus fare to meet up with friends, and the cost of childcare was prohibitive for those with pre-school children or those wanting to participate in any adult activities outside of school hours. The demands on time both of parenting and managing on a low income (see Chapter 3) were also important constraints, especially for lone parents and those families in which either parent or child had a health problem that required regular doctor or health visitor appointments. Poverty-related stigma combined with many other sources of stigma (see Chapter 3) also contributed to social isolation for many, making them wary of new encounters. Many parents had established friendships with others in similar circumstances to them partly in response to stigma, but where it remained a barrier to developing new friendships they were very vulnerable to isolation if conflict or mobility interrupted old friendships.

Poverty-related stigma and restrictions were cited as a particularly significant barrier by those who had dropped into poverty and whose previously established social networks involved people on higher incomes. These parents were no longer able to participate in the same types of social activities as their friends (e.g. going out to eat, or a concert or show). When these friends made efforts to continue to include them by finding cheaper activities or subsidising them, parents often experienced these efforts as humiliating. One woman spoke of meeting up with her university friends having made a special effort to save up enough to buy one round of drinks, but then finding her friends would not allow her to buy her round. Although it was never said, she knew this was because she was now living in poverty and, unable to bear the implied difference, she had left early and had not seen them since.

As has been found in previous research (Pantazis and Ruspini, 2006), men had fewer supportive friends than women and about half of the men in the study had no friends in their support network. Men mostly confided in and got emotional support from their partners or family members and, while most had some interest-sharing friends, they said they would never discuss personal or family issues with them. A couple of men were recovering from drug addictions and it seemed they had separated themselves from previous groups of friends because they were associated with a drug-using culture. Neither had formed any new friendships.

A few parents seemed to have lost friends over the years because they had experienced repeated traumas throughout their lives and had only managed to maintain relationships with family. They expressed a sense of being united with their family (often just a small number) against outsiders and having given up on trying to establish and maintain friendships.

Perhaps surprisingly, parents who had experienced domestic violence had the same size of support networks as other parents. Domestic violence often involves social isolation (from friends and family) as part of a pattern of control (Mullender, 1996; Hanmer and Itzin, 2001) and many described this as part of their past experience. However, all had now left the violent relationships and most had rebuilt a social network since doing so. While most mothers who had experienced domestic violence did not include their ex-partner in their support network, there were a small number who did. The support given was invariably in the form of care for the children (and hence helpful respite for the mother), and usually the mother was in a situation where she no longer felt threatened by her ex-partner. Mothers who still had contact with violent ex-partners because those partners had legal access to their children, but who did still feel threatened by or continued to experience some ongoing emotional abuse from these ex-partners rarely included them in their support networks even when the childcare might be a respite.

Ghate and Hazel (2002) found that lone parents had smaller support networks than those from two-parent households. This study, however, found no difference in the size of support networks. In fact lone parents tended to have both more supportive friends and more interest-sharing friends than parents from two-parent households. This was true both for immigrant parents (who tended to have fewer friends anyway) and for other parents. It seemed that the parents with partners in this study were particularly dependent on their partner for support. Although it is difficult to know quite why this should be, it may be the result of the particularly high levels of adversity, both past and present, and service intervention in our sample. Parents who have experienced high levels of trauma, who are involved with potentially stigmatising services and who have a resident partner from whom they receive strong support within the home may rely more on that partner relationship, preferring to keep the processes of dealing with personal traumas within the home.

IMPACTS OF INFORMAL SUPPORT NETWORKS ON PARENTING

When parents had support from their own parents, this could involve a very substantial contribution to parenting, particularly when parents had a good, emotionally supportive relationship with their parents and therefore felt able to ask parents for any help they needed and to rely on it. In such contexts, they had access to considerable practical and financial support, which was almost never available from any other source. Practical and financial support did not usually need to be reciprocated, although the emotional support in good relationships was usually mutual. Regular free childcare could give them respite and allow them to get housework done, attend medical or counselling appointments, or work or study part time. Financial contributions usually came in the form of paying for things rather than cash contributions, most often gifts to the children (clothes, uniforms, toys, sports or music equipment, days out, classes), sometimes gifts to a parent (e.g. clothes) and also things for the family as a whole (e.g. family holidays, car running costs). Grandparents also contributed food, particularly when parents were short of money and waiting for their next benefit payment, sometimes by inviting the family over to eat and sometimes by bringing food to them. Even when grandparents might not have the financial means to buy very much, they would often still buy regular treats for the children and have them over to eat.

Some parents who had poor relationships with their own parents still received some support, but it was both more restricted and more mixed in impact. These parents often felt unable to ask for things they or their children needed unless they were offered. Help that was given was also sometimes felt to impose an obligation, which they were uncomfortable with or unable to meet. In a few cases, a form of financial abuse seemed to occur, with financial involvement by grandparents being a means of control over the parent.

The emotional and moral support from supportive friendships was particularly important to many mothers (and a few fathers). Some women described having a group of good friends who lived in similar circumstances and organised their social lives to accommodate the restrictions they shared, visiting each other at home rather than going out (often during the day when children were at school), meeting at free activities or seeking out sales or cheap deals to attend together. These women supported each other in their daily difficulties and reinforced a positive self-image for each other as parents who were doing well despite adversity. Not all women had a whole group of friends, but most had at least one with whom they formed a mutually supportive relationship. Women often described these relationships as 'life-saving', allowing them to de-stress and get their worries in perspective, and thus supporting their parenting.

Parents often shared interests and did activities unrelated to parenting with friends they also got support from. Some also had interest-sharing friends with whom they did not discuss personal issues or support. Purely interest-sharing friends were less common and only 38 per cent of parents had any, poverty being cited as the main barrier, as parents could rarely afford to go out and socialise. Interest-sharing friends are often not included in studies of social networks (e.g. Ghate and Hazel, 2002), but may play a significant part in maintaining well-being (Heard and Lake, 1986, 1997). For a few parents in our study, interest-sharing friends were extremely important, offering time out and positive experiences that helped them cope better with the stresses in the rest of their lives. It was often important to them that these friends did not know of the difficulties they were experiencing at home because it allowed them to leave these problems and any stigma associated with them behind.

There was some degree of crossover between informal and more formal support networks in that parents often felt they had personal friendships with professionals who worked with them. This was more common in relationships with professionals from non-statutory services (including support workers from charities for lone parents, for women experiencing domestic violence and for low-income families in social housing) but did sometimes include those from statutory services. These relationships are discussed in Chapter 6.

BEYOND POVERTY *OR* PARENTING: TOWARDS THE ECOLOGICAL MODEL

In elaborating the other forms of adversity experienced by the families in our sample, we do not wish to divert attention from the many ways poverty itself impacts on family life, of which numerous examples have been given in the last two chapters. Both lack of resources and the time, energy and worry involved in managing lives filled with uncertainty meant parents sometimes lacked the resources to meet children's basic needs, for food, clean clothes, attention, stimulating activities and opportunities for play with friends. Scarce resources (money, time and space) could generate competition and conflict between family members. Loss of independent income and enforced dependency could place too much pressure on new partnerships. A sense of failure in their own lives could undermine parents' efforts to influence their children's behaviour. Some parents had managed to sustain rewarding family relationships despite poverty but the challenges of doing so should not be underestimated.

Many of the issues covered in this chapter are by no means exclusive to poverty – child maltreatment, domestic violence, rape, mental health problems, relationship breakdown, children's behaviour problems all occur across socio-economic groups. While some are made more likely to occur by poverty (e.g. mothers' depression, children's behaviour problems), they are all made harder to live with by poverty, with the constant pressure on resources and restricted options for accessing help (therapeutic, legal or social support), relief from responsibilities (childcare), or distraction (activities and treats for children and time out for parents) it entails. Some also make poverty more difficult to manage, for example via the ongoing effects of childhood maltreatment or domestic violence on confidence and support networks, and the compounding effects of different sources of stigma. While focusing on these other issues in research sometimes allows poverty to slip out of sight, the multiple sources of adversity are inseparable to those who live them.

At the time of writing, the appointment of 'parenting experts' (dubbed 'supernannies' by the press) to help parents in 77 deprived areas control anti-social children has just been announced, in response partly to the widespread public perception that 'bad parenting is responsible for bad behaviour' (Weaver, 2006). Although help is intended to be voluntary if possible, options for the use of compulsion, requiring parents to undertake parenting classes through parenting orders, are also being extended. Clearly many parents, not only those in deprived areas, lack confidence in parenting and would value more help and advice. Equally clearly, there are many factors that contribute to anti-social behaviour, of which parenting is only one, however important. Other initiatives focus on neighbourhood deprivation of course, recognising that children's 'bad behaviour' may be influenced as much by peer group norms, other local role models and lack of opportunities. But debate about such developments easily focuses around oversimplistic dichotomies – is it poverty and deprived neighbourhoods or parenting that is the problem? A recent, more extensive UK study than ours, however, concluded that individual, family and neighbourhood factors needed to be considered together, since it was the interactions between parents, families and their neighbourhoods that were of crucial importance in influencing children's behaviour (Barnes and Cheng, 2006).

When asked what would make most difference to their lives, many parents in our study said more money or better housing. Others wanted help to resolve the impacts of traumatic experiences for themselves and/or their children. Those experiencing difficulties in parenting also wanted more help to manage their children (as do many parents across all income levels) and we discuss their experiences of seeking it in Chapter 6. Advice on parenting may well be of limited use, however, if it ignores parents' own needs and/or fails to recognise the context in which they parent. Indeed, as the use of compulsion to educate parents spreads, there is a real risk of increasing the alienation of parents who are well used to experiencing more trouble than support in their lives, distrustful of authority and struggling in what many perceive as unjustly difficult circumstances.

We end this chapter with the words of a parent in a deprived area.

> I: *If you could tell Tony Blair about if you could make your life better, what would you say ... last question?*
>
> R: *Mr Blair, Dear Mr Blair, make my life better bloody hell don't keep casting a brick across my head just because my kids are having it hard in school, I don't have no money, I'm not working don't put me in that category with everybody else and low lives, you know low lives, I ain't a bloody low life. You, Mr Blair get your nice cushy household and you lovely and you protected from the street shit come here and let your kids cope here for a week and then you can see how you get on with your kids. See if your kids are so calm and cool and nice and sit down in the corner and behave. I bet you they don't ... I bet you they don't but you try to keep straight and healthy and happy and nice. You try and deal with them kids that like Mr Blair's lifestyle. That's too boring for my kids. So you see how are you going to teach these kids your way ... you way. Cause I don't have your money Mr Blair and I don't have your posh schools, Mr Blair. I have shitty [local gang] that's it. You know, how am I gonna do it.*

NOTES

1. A figure of around 7–7.5 per cent is typically found in nationally representative samples such as the National Child Development Study (http://www.cls.ioe.ac.uk/studies. asp?section=000100020003).

2. The three parenting styles we refer to here are from a typology developed by Baumrind (1967). In brief, an authoritative parent tends to exercise authority using reasoning, rewards and a consistent regime, while also listening to and engaging with the child's perspective. A permissive parent tends to avoid exercising control or setting standards, allowing the child to regulate their own activities. An authoritarian parent tends actively to try to shape the child's behaviour to preconceived standards, and may use punitive discipline to do so. Like most typologies, it captures a useful distinction, while also leaving out much of the complexity, variability and range of parenting behaviour. Different styles may be adopted by the same parent in different contexts and may also have a different meaning and impact in different cultural contexts.

5 Growing up in a low-income household – children's experiences and well-being

KEY POINTS

- Children as young as five had a range of worries, sometimes very serious, about their families' circumstances.

- Children were most often stressed by their parents being stressed. Many knew that poverty was a key source of that stress, and tried to alleviate it by hiding their needs and wishes and/or giving or lending money they had received from other family members. They were also often sad, angry, frustrated or upset by the impacts of poverty on their lives.

- Children's relationships with their families and friends were central to their experience and well-being, and were sources of stress or unhappiness for some and resilience for others.

- Conflict within the home, siblings with behaviour problems, difficult relationships with non-resident parents and bullying within peer groups were key sources of unhappiness for children. Bullying was often clearly related to poverty for children living in affluent areas. Children in deprived areas had the additional stress of a more violent local culture, including gangs using weapons in schools and the community.

- Mothers, siblings and friends were most consistently mentioned in children's social networks. Mothers were the key support figures. Relationships with siblings and friends were also highly valued, and friends could offer important protection against bullying.

- Grandparents were also important, especially where there was conflict with parents. As many children said they would talk to their grandmother if they had a problem as said they would talk to their father. Where available, grandparents played a key role in caregiving for children and support for parents. Nearly half the children had no grandparents in their social network, however, mainly because of either past maltreatment of their parents resulting in estrangement or distance (often related to immigration).

- Absence of or unreliable care from a non-resident parent had impacts akin to a form of emotional abuse. Disputes over contact with non-resident parents were very stressful for children. Some had had their expressed preferences overridden by courts, creating extreme distress. A few retained lasting fears of being forced to be with violent fathers again, even if contact had subsequently stopped.

- Behaviour problems were often clearly related to trauma or stress. They were exacerbated by overcrowded housing and lack of resources for therapy or counselling for traumatised children, respite care to give parents or siblings a break, and activities

(Continued)

for children. Boys scored worse than girls on behavioural difficulties, hyperactivity, lack of kind and helpful behaviour, and overall difficulties or stress.

- Poverty impacted on children's well-being in a range of ways relevant to each of the dimensions used in current definitions.

- Children's aspirations for their future at this age (five to 11) often remained high. If they fail to fulfil their potential later, as the evidence on disadvantage being perpetuated across generations suggests may be the case, the emotional impacts of living in often unsafe and uncertain environments, and the learnt response of trying to protect others from their needs and wishes, are likely to be contributing factors.

This chapter deals in depth with the data collected from the interviews with children aged five to 11 years and details their experiences and views. It also draws on the parents' accounts of their children's lives, including the scores derived from the Strengths and Difficulties Questionnaire (SDQ) filled in by parents. Some information on the lives of older and younger siblings is also gained from both children's and parents' descriptions of family life. The first section looks at the sources of stress and resilience in children's lives as identified by the children themselves, largely situated within their key relationships. While much of this is familiar from previous research with children, these are a younger group – around a third of them aged five to seven, the rest eight to 11. The second section gives a brief summary of the relevance of poverty to the five outcomes identified in *Every Child Matters* (HM Government, 2004), based on the findings from this study. Finally, in the light of our findings, we discuss the issue of how disadvantage may be passed on from generation to generation.

STRESS AND RESILIENCE: CHILDREN'S EXPERIENCES

The sources of stress in children's lives in many ways echoed those in their parents' lives, described in the last two chapters. Children were distressed by things they could not do or have because of poverty, and the effect this had on their social relationships, at home and at school. They were also affected by overcrowded housing and associated conflicts, lack of privacy and sleep, by poor housing conditions that affected their health, by worries about the health and safety of other family members (especially in the aftermath of domestic violence), and by violence and crime in the community, among other issues. Some examples of children's accounts of the stresses that poverty created for them and the range of worries (sometimes very serious) they had are given in the box below.

CHILDREN'S ACCOUNTS OF SOURCES OF STRESS OR WORRY

A girl aged eight in a two-parent, five-child family wholly dependent on benefits and with debts of over £30,000 was afraid her baby sister could die because the family found it very hard to afford enough food:

I: *How do you feel about not having much money?*

R: *Well really, really scared.*

I: *Scared, why scared?*

(Continued)

R: *Because if we don't have much money then we won't buy food and then Melissa will die.*

A girl aged nine, whose family had relocated to escape her father's domestic violence, and whose mother was very stressed primarily by living in poverty now, described feeling ill with worry about her family:

I'm always ill, cos I have like worries in my tummy and stuff.

A girl aged 11 described how the circumstances in her household – a combination of poverty, debt, mum's ill-health, and the girls' disability – made her feel:

I: *How does [stress] feel, give me three words, what does stress feel like?*

R: *[It] makes you feel angry, it makes you feel sad, down and, and tired and stuff.*

A nine-year-old boy described how he would try and joke with his mother to cheer her up when he was aware she was feeling stressed about lack of money, but sometimes she would get angry and shout at him in response and he would feel sad that he had upset her:

I: *Can you tell me about a time when, when you were teasing her and she shouted at you and then you felt sad?*

R: *I was trying to have a joke with her but, and saying, oh I forgot what it was but I joked to her about something and then I tried to make, I was just trying to make her laugh and she was quite stressed because she like had no money at that moment and she said, she said stuff like 'Go up to your room now' and 'Would you stop it please' and 'I don't like the way you joke with me most of the time' and stuff. But I was only trying to make her feel better instead of being stressed.*

A nine-year-old girl who witnessed her stepfather trying to strangle her mother described how she still feels unsafe in her own home and afraid for her family:

R: *It's all going a bit wrong and we have, we used to have … a stepdad … and [he] tried to hurt my mum and kill her and that and [he's] actually been in prison for it … and I don't be, and I'm certain but I'm not that certain about our, my family.*

I: *What do you mean you're not that certain, how do you feel?*

R: *A bit scared because if they can climb up onto the wheelie bin and then onto the bit that's on top of our door they can easily climb into my window. So at night-times they make me feel a bit scared because my window doesn't actually shut properly but now we've fixed it, it's done but it isn't actually locked properly yet because I don't think we can find the key. So it's really, it's really scary for me.*

(Continued)

> A ten-year-old boy whose mother was sectioned following a psychotic incident worries about her getting ill again and going into hospital:
>
> *I'm worried about my mum going back in hospital and stuff like that.*
>
> His mother described how he would check on her in the night, getting up to make sure she was still safely in bed. He worried about her being stressed and had bought her a country and western CD, which she would fall asleep to:
>
> [When mum is stressed it] *makes me like feel unhappy inside cos, cos if she's stressed then there's nowt that I can do about it.*

Many children talked of feeling sad about being poor, and some went on to describe how it made them feel anxious, frightened, frustrated and/or angry. A couple of children also said it made them want to get away from their homes, although, for the vast majority, family relationships were central to their resilience, as well as a major source of stress and unhappiness where there were problems. Almost all children liked going to school, seeing their friends there and doing the subjects they were good at or found enjoyable (often because of a well-liked teacher). Those who did not like school mostly either had serious behavioural problems, and regularly got into trouble, or were bullied at school. Many of those who were bullied still liked some aspects of school (often learning or a particular teacher) but wanted to go to a school where they were not bullied. There were also a few children who did not dislike anything about school but who disliked being away from their families because they were afraid of what might happen in their absence. These included families where a parent had been hospitalised for physical or mental health problems and where a mother had been the victim of domestic violence in the past.

Children's relationships, most importantly those within their immediate family but also extended family, their own friends and their parents' friends, were central to their experience of poverty and to their well-being. The most frequently mentioned cause of their own stress was parents' stress, often recognised to be the result of poverty, but also including realistic concerns about parents' health and vulnerability to violence. Poverty and other related factors such as poor housing caused children distress partly because of the deprivations entailed for them directly, partly because the demands on their parents interfered with their ability to respond to children's needs, but also because, even at this age, children worried a good deal about their parents. Conflicts within the home (involving any combination of parents, siblings or self) were another common source of stress and distress. When there was a sibling with behavioural problems, this could be a source of stress or unhappiness if the behavioural problems involved aggression or violence against the child or created conflict in the home. Where the relationship with a non-resident parent was difficult or the experience of care from that parent was poor, this was a key source of unhappiness for those children.

Relationships with peers and sometimes with a wider network of family friends were also a key source of resilience for children who had good friendships and a source of unhappiness for those who lacked them. Outside of the family, the most commonly mentioned source of stress or unhappiness was bullying (almost always in school). Bullying was mentioned much more frequently by children in affluent areas than children in deprived areas. Several children in affluent areas described what was clearly poverty-related bullying – being told they were dirty or had nasty habits because they came from a poor family, or that they would always be poor because their parents were poor. Only children in deprived areas, however, cited the more generalised threat of violence, crime and intimidation by gangs in schools and neighbourhoods, which was a major source of stress for them.

The extent and quality of relationships in children's social networks were a key source of resilience. However, most of the families in this sample had experienced the kind of traumas that often result in family fragmentation and estrangement, as was discussed in the last chapter. The number of people in the children's social networks ranged from three to 34, with an average of ten. Members of the children's social networks included mothers, fathers, step-parents, grandparents, uncles, aunties, cousins, friends their own age, adult friends who were usually friends of their parents, family pets, occasionally teachers and once a social worker. The combinations varied widely but only mothers, friends their own age and siblings if they had any were consistently included in children's social networks. Typically, children's social networks included their mother, one to five friends and one to five other relatives (most often siblings if present and then grandparents).

PARENT–CHILD RELATIONSHIPS

Resident parents were almost always included in children's social networks (all resident mothers and some resident fathers and stepfathers). Mothers were the key support figures. Almost all children said they would talk to their mothers if they had a problem or were worried about something and half of the children would confide only in their mothers. Just three children said they would not talk to their mum but to a different family member. For the two where the mother was resident, their main source of worry was their mother's health. Of the children who were resident with their biological father, only just over half would go to their father as well as their mother, with no difference between girls and boys, but none of the six children with resident stepfathers said they would go to them with worries. Just under a third of children with non-resident dads who were part of their social network would also talk to them about worries or problems. Overall, only 21 per cent would turn to their fathers or stepfathers.

Nationally representative surveys of older children or young people have found that 40 per cent of children would turn to fathers as well as mothers and that boys were twice as likely as girls to go to their fathers with problems (Cawson *et al.*, 2000; Park *et al.*, 2004). While mothers tend to be the preferred person for children to turn to, and especially so for younger children (Gorin, 2004), fathers in this sample were both less available (when non-resident and sometimes absent from the child's life) and had not always provided good experiences of care.

Poverty-related stress: impacts on children and their response

Parents being stressed was the factor mentioned most frequently by children as a cause of their own stress or unhappiness. Most children spoke of feeling sad, many stressed, some angry, and a few afraid, bored or helpless when their parents were stressed. Several children worried that their parents would become ill because of stress, a realistic concern given the high levels of mental health problems among parents.

An analysis of the measures of parental stress levels (malaise scores) and child stress levels (SDQ) indicated that children's stress levels were significantly higher if their parents were stressed but that children's stress (or lack of it) had little impact on parents' stress levels, rather these were affected by a wider range of factors.[1] This indicates that stress experienced by the parents, which might not necessarily be expected to affect children directly (e.g. concerns around payment of bills or debts, worries about the future) was being passed on to children, whether or not they fully understood the causes.

Although some children appeared to have little idea why their parents might be stressed or unhappy, many were aware that one of the main sources of stress for their parents was poverty. Some children described how they tried to help reduce poverty-related stress for their parents by limiting what they asked for, including keeping school trips secret from parents because they did not want them to have the worry of paying for them or to face the stress of having to decide whether they could be afforded. At the same time, children were also upset by the deprivation, and by missing out on experiences and things their friends had:

> R: *I just really want a little bit more pocket money cos I mean at Christmas my mum has to get, she has to like spend in 1p coins cos she hardly has enough and she really has to fork out to get enough money like for toys and stuff, I sometimes say 'Just get me one little present' and at my birthday, it's coming up now, I said 'I'll save up to get a Nintendo' but she's going to help me out a little bit and I don't really feel a little bit happy about that, cos she doesn't really have enough money to get it, so I find it really upsetting.*

> I: *So you're worried that she won't be able to afford it?*

> R: *Yeah, and I find it really upsetting because I'm just like going to get just that little one thing and I just think I should really be paying for stuff, I should do more for my mum that I'm not doing really, but I don't really have enough money to do any more.*

(Girl, eight years)

All of the children interviewed were under 12 and none worked for money, but several families reported older children, some as young as 12, working (e.g. paper rounds or gardening for neighbours) and contributing money to household bills. Younger children would sometimes give or lend parents money (or offer to) from their piggy banks, or money they had received from non-resident parents or grandparents to help with household expenses.

Non-resident parents: quality of care as key stress or source of resilience

Whether non-resident fathers were included in children's social networks or not seemed to depend both on the quality of the relationship and on the importance the child placed on that relationship. Children would include fathers when they had a good relationship and regular contact, but also sometimes when they had very little contact and an unsatisfactory relationship but aspired to a better experience of care from their father. Other children with similarly poor experiences of care from non-resident parents appeared to have given up on this relationship, and some had rejected contact with a previously abusive father.

When children had a poor relationship or experience of care from a non-resident parent, this was always a key source of stress or unhappiness for them. Since most children were resident with their mothers, almost all non-resident parents were fathers, but our sample did include three families with non-resident mothers, all of whom provided poor care to some extent and children appeared to feel very similarly about poor care from both non-resident mothers and fathers. Several children spoke of feeling abandoned by their non-resident parent: '*I don't see my Dad though, cos he never bothers*' (girl aged ten). Even when they had regular contact with their non-resident parent, they did not necessarily feel cared for by them, describing feeling ignored when they went to stay, or feeling of secondary importance compared to the parent's new family. Unreliability was a common theme, with non-resident parents cancelling or simply failing to turn up to collect children for prearranged visits and also failing to call or answer calls even when they had bought their child a mobile phone expressly to enhance contact. In some families, non-resident parents seemed to disappear from their children's lives for weeks or even months without explanation. These absences (whether long- or short-term), unreliability and unavailability (both physical and emotional) of non-resident parents are clearly very upsetting for children. The impact seems akin to the 'withdrawal' or 'withholding of affection and care' that Cawson *et al.* (2000) include in their definition of emotional abuse, although absence of care from a non-resident parent is not usually included in such definitions. However, for most of these children, non-resident parents appear to have a very important role in their emotional and psychological well-being and therefore have potential to do significant harm.

In some families, the poor experience of care from non-resident fathers (but not mothers) also involved (or had in the past involved) physical and emotional abuse, including domestic violence. Some of the children who had witnessed or were aware of domestic violence by their absent father against their mother had mixed feelings about their father, wanting to maintain a relationship but fearing a repeat of earlier abuse, sometimes expressing concern for the absent father. Other children felt very strongly that they didn't want to have contact with their fathers, including both children who had been directly abused by their fathers and those who had not but had witnessed domestic violence against their mothers. For this latter group, fear for themselves or their mother was often a substantial source of current stress even though they might have had no contact with the father for several years.

Several families described very stressful periods, when violent fathers had sought access to or custody of children after separating from their mother, when those children were afraid of their father and didn't want contact.[2] Often the past history of abuse and/or domestic violence was only reported to professionals during the custody dispute, was contested by the father and was sometimes therefore treated with scepticism by the professionals involved. The views of three children had apparently been discounted, either by attributing their wish to have no contact with their fathers to their mother's influence or by explaining their accounts of violence as acceptable discipline. This may well have been because of their young age, which ranged from seven to 11. One woman was aware that, once her daughter was 12, she would be able to refuse contact on her own behalf. Children should not be left waiting until they grow older, however, for their views to be heard and their safety protected. Both mothers and children described the extreme distress of children when they felt they would be forced to spend time with the father they feared. Even when contact arrangements had subsequently broken down and the child had had no contact with the father for several years, some children were still afraid that someone would force them to be with their father.

A few non-resident fathers in this sample had positive relationships with their children and provided good experiences of care. These relationships tended to be characterised by a high degree of availability and reliability by the father, with regular visits and phone calls, and children having a sense that they could contact their father whenever they wished. Occasionally, non-resident fathers had even achieved some form of shared care that was supportive of both child and resident parent. In families where siblings had different non-resident fathers, they sometimes had very different experiences of them, which could contribute to resentment and conflict within the family.

Children with behavioural problems

Of the children interviewed, 42 per cent scored high or very high for behavioural problems on the SDQ and 69 per cent scored high or very high for at least one element of difficulty. This is far higher than was found by Ghate and Hazel (2002) in their nationally representative sample of low-income families, where only 13 per cent of children were found to have abnormally high SDQ difficulties scores. In addition, parents reported behavioural problems in children other than the one who was interviewed and so the number of families with a child with behavioural problems is higher. Given the sample families were selected in order to include a large number with a history of child maltreatment, and the high levels of domestic violence experienced by women (see Chapter 4), it is not surprising that there are also high levels of child behavioural problems. Exposure to family violence, both as victim and observer, is associated with externalising behavioural problems in children (Sternberg *et al.*, 2006). When a child had behavioural problems, this usually put a degree of strain on the parent–child relationship, although both the nature of the behaviour and the way in which the parent responded affected the degree of negative effect on their relationship.

The range of issues covered by the term behaviour problems was described in the last chapter. Of the children interviewed, 18 per cent had behaviour problems of the severe kind, involving aggressive and violent behaviour. The remaining 24 per cent had regular conflicts with their parents, sometimes involving aggression, though the frequency varied and there were sometimes also times of shared happiness in the relationship. The second group included all but one of the families with children currently on the CPR, and also some families where the child in question had a particularly difficult meaning for the parent (e.g, where the child had been conceived by rape). For the other family with children currently on the CPR, the incident concerned sexual abuse by a member of the extended family rather than parent–child conflict and the interviewed child from that family had close to normal scores for all SDQ measures, although the mother reported that her sons were easily scared. The SDQ scores represent only the perspective of the parents, usually only one parent, and there is some evidence that abusive parents may over-report externalising behaviour problems in their children (Lau *et al.*, 2006). However, in most accounts from parents and children, there was strong supporting evidence for the behavioural problems described.

There were statistically significant differences between girls and boys in the scores, both for behavioural problems and for some other difficulties measured by the SDQ.[3] Boys scored worse than girls on behavioural difficulties, hyperactivity, lack of kind and helpful behaviour, and overall difficulties or stress. This may be partly because boys respond to trauma and stress with the types of externalising behavioural problems that are most apparent to parents, whereas girls respond with less apparent or disruptive internalising behaviour. In a study that compared the reporting of behavioural problems by caregivers and by children, Rosenthal and Curiel (2006) found that, although caregivers reported higher levels for boys than for girls, the girls self-reported higher levels than the boys, partly because their problems were under-recognised and partly because they were more critical of their own behaviour. In our study, there were several girls who scored normal or close to normal on the SDQ but who described being very distressed by family circumstances, worried about their parents (usually their mother) and making special efforts to care for their parent with practical help around the house and by hiding their own worries. Other research has found that, while boys may develop anti-social behavioural problems in childhood, girls tend to develop such problems only in adolescence (Silverthorn and Frick, 1999). Since all the children interviewed are under 12, it may also be that, while both boys and girls' behaviour will be negatively affected by the trauma and stress they have experienced, as yet only the boys' problems are apparent. Children in the deprived contexts also scored significantly worse on kind and helpful behaviour than those in the affluent context sample. This difference may reflect the influence of their unsafe environments, either via the modelling of anti-social behaviour in the community or via defensive reactions to fear.

Poverty may contribute to child behavioural problems as well as making them more difficult to deal with. Longer exposure to poverty in early childhood is associated with greater child behavioural problems in middle childhood (Hao and Matsueda, 2006), partly because it undermines parents' ability to care for their children and to facilitate the crucial socialisation stage of children transitioning from infancy to early childhood (Duncan *et al.*, 1994; Duncan and Brooks-Gunn, 1997). In addition, this research suggests that children's worries about their parents' stress and its impacts on them may contribute to their difficulties from a relatively young age. Poverty also meant parents could not afford any kinds of private services, whether counselling for traumatised children or respite care to give themselves or the siblings a break, or many activities or distractions for children. These families often spent large amount of times at home, none of them able to escape the stress of the situation. The impact of this was particularly severe for those families living in overcrowded conditions.

SIBLING RELATIONSHIPS

When present, siblings were almost always included in children's social networks and those of a similar age were frequent playmates at home and in the neighbourhood, while older siblings were sometimes role models and often gave children access to activities or treats they would not otherwise have. Sibling relationships are important for child well-being and positive sibling relationships have been linked to greater social competence (Pike *et al.*, 2006). Children valued their relationships with their siblings and, even when there was some element of conflict in the relationship, they usually emphasised the positive aspects and wished away the difficulties.

Siblings with behavioural problems

When a child had a sibling with behavioural problems, they often expressed sympathy for and a desire to support their sibling while also finding their behavioural problems a source of stress. In most families where a child had some behavioural problems, these led to increased conflicts and family stress, took up a disproportionate amount of parents' time and attention, and limited family participation in activities outside of the home. All of these varied in degree and therefore in impacts on children – the more frequent, extreme and aggressive the problems, the greater the negative impacts on siblings. In a few families, the child with behavioural problems was aggressive and occasionally violent towards his or her siblings and this had a severe impact on children who were subject to it.

Violent and aggressive behaviour from siblings with behavioural problems included regular physical violence resulting in bruising, often constant verbal abuse and threats towards siblings and parents, and destruction of household and sibling possessions, which could be ill afforded by these families: '*I swear when he goes like angry he just hits … he throws, I swear … and I used to have this big massive bruise up there cos he kicked me … he always does stuff like this*' (girl, 11 years, referring to her twin brother). The brother said he didn't like his sister and it appeared he was deliberately targeting his aggression against her. The girl didn't feel there was any point talking to her mother about the problem because '*nothing can be done*' and instead would go to her bedroom and cry. In another family, a 12-year-old girl was constantly hitting or pinching her siblings. Her six-year-old sister said '*she hurts me all the time*' and the girl's behaviour had contributed to her 16-year-old brother's decision to move out of the family home and into supported accommodation. The impacts of an aggressive and violent sibling's behavioural problems on a child were emotional as well as physical, particularly when the aggression was directed at that child. In one family, a 15-year-old boy had kept his mum, 13-year-old sister and six-year-old brother trapped upstairs for several hours while he threatened them with a knife. In another family, where the recently departed father had been emotionally and physically abusive towards mum and children, the ten-year-old daughter had developed aggressive and violent behavioural problems, which included very controlling behaviour towards her mum and to a lesser extent her two older sisters (16 and 13 years). She closely policed and limited the time her mum spent with her older sisters and prevented them spending time together in the family rooms; her older sisters tended to keep to their own rooms.

In other families, violent behaviour was more of a risk to the child concerned than their siblings, where, for example, the child was younger and/or slighter in build than his or her siblings and attacks had little impact, or the child self-harmed. Such incidents and children who put themselves at risk (e.g. by running away) were still mentioned as sources of stress by siblings, both because of the stress caused to parents and because of the child's own concern for their brother or sister.

EXTENDED FAMILY: THE IMPORTANCE OF GRANDPARENTS

Grandparents were included by 53 per cent of the children, usually maternal grandparents and most often the maternal grandmother, but in some cases up to five grandparents (including some stepgrandparents). When present, grandparents, particularly grandmothers, often played a key caregiving role. Many grandparents were providing regular childcare, either at the family home or by having grandchildren to stay with them. Grandparents provided emotional support to their grandchildren, which was particularly important in families where there was parent–child conflict or where children did not want to discuss their own worries with their parents for fear of adding to their parents' stress. Twenty-one per cent of children said that they would talk to their grandmother if they were worried or had a problem; usually this was in addition to mum, but three children said they would only talk to their grandmother. In addition, many grandparents gave their grandchildren access to activities and experiences (e.g. day trips, holidays, lessons or activities with friends), which they wouldn't otherwise have because their parents couldn't afford them. Activities with grandparents also included doing craft activities and playing outside, which were not necessarily expensive but which some parents did not do with their children because of health problems and/or lack of time or energy.

A smaller proportion of children (41 per cent) included other family members in their social networks, typically one to four aunts or uncles and one to three cousins. The role of these other family members varied greatly, in terms both of frequency of contact and of the activities involved. Children often greatly valued their relationships with other family members but they did not play the same role as those with grandparents in giving children access to additional activities and experiences or the same level of emotional support. Only rarely did a child say they might talk to an aunt or adult sibling if they had a problem.

Almost half (47 per cent) of the children had no grandparents in their social network and there were two main reasons for this. Where their parents and grandparents were estranged and had little or no contact because of past maltreatment or poor care, both parents and children were sometimes estranged from other extended family members too. In families where children still had contact with grandparents despite their parent's history of maltreatment from them (see Chapter 4), it seemed more difficult for children to receive emotional support from these grandparents and the child–grandparent relationship was sometimes a source of conflict or a difficult area in the parent–child relationship. Where grandparents lived too far away to play an active role in their lives (often overseas), there was regular contact by phone, which children valued, but these overseas family members were able to play little practical role in children's lives.

The social networks of parents clearly had a strong influence over their children's social networks at this age, particularly over the family members included, and resident parents had a much greater influence than non-resident parents. Parents' friendships also influenced which adults were potential adult friends for children. While they had less influence over children's friendships with peers, some parents may have limited these where their fears for their children's safety or about the potential bad influence of local children meant they did not allow their children to play outside with friends from the neighbourhood.

FRIENDSHIPS

Children's friendships with peers were very important to them. Ninety-three per cent of children included at least one friend in their social network, typically two to five. Children differentiated between 'best' friends who they could trust and rely on and other friends who they enjoyed being with, the former being more highly valued. Several children said they would talk to their best friend if they had any worries. These categories correspond to friends who provide support and interest-sharing friends in adult social networks. For some children, poverty was a barrier to having friends, while, for others, friends were a shield against the disadvantages of poverty. Several children described how they did not feel their relative poverty put them at a social disadvantage because they had 'good friends'. In affluent areas, children's friends were often from relatively better-off families but the children who had strong friendships said this did not affect their friendship or what they did together. They sometimes reported friends sharing resources (e.g. money to spend on a shopping trip, toys children would not otherwise get to try) and friends' families including them in outings they would not normally get to do with their own families. This latter is reminiscent of adult 'bridging' friendships, which have been linked to routes out of poverty (Fitzpatrick, 2004). Although friendships made in primary school may not persist into adult life, the social skills and models for protective and possibly bridging friendships may give these children great advantages in later life.

Around a quarter (26 per cent) of children included adult friends in their social networks. These were usually adult friends of their parents (most frequently female friends of their mothers) who were included in both parent and child social networks and had a family friend role. Often the adult was the parent of one of the child's friends and the mothers had met through their children and become part of each other's social networks. Children also included regular babysitters as adult friends and a couple of children included other adults from the neighbourhood with whom they were friendly. The main shared activity with adult friends was simply being together, visiting with each other, playing and talking. These family friends often had a similar role to extended family members but were not a source of emotional support in the same way that their grandmother could be; no child said they would go to a family friend with their worries.

Children with behavioural problems included friends, particularly best friends, much less often than other children and had a lower number of friends in their social networks on average. Lack of friends contributed to children's current stress and unhappiness and, in the longer term, lack of social competency is likely to be a significant disadvantage. Interestingly, over a third of children with the most extreme behavioural problems included pets in their social networks, while only 9 per cent of other children did. It appears that, where children are less able to form relationships with peers, animals may offer a more easily negotiated substitute. Lack of friends may have contributed to the particularly difficult time at school experienced by children with behavioural problems – some of the interviewees in the under-12 age group had already been excluded from one school. Externalising problems in childhood undermine academic competence by adolescence and are linked to negative academic and job outcomes (Masten *et al.*, 2005; Gest *et al.*, 2006).

Bullying, violence and the protective influence of friendships

One of the main ways in which poverty was a key stress for the children was in the stigma they experienced among peers and related bullying. Bullying in school was mentioned by a third of children from affluent areas but only 11 per cent of children from deprived areas. Although this is not a representative sample, being a smaller and visibly different minority may make poor children more vulnerable to bullying in such contexts. However, weapons and violent assaults in school (not necessarily against the children interviewed) were mentioned more frequently by children from deprived areas. This violence and intimidation, which was a significant source of stress for some children in deprived areas, did not appear to be connected primarily to bullying but to be part of local culture, often influenced by gangs. Those children who are bullied in such a context may be at greater risk of injury than children in affluent areas.

A few children talked about keeping their relative poverty hidden by avoiding bringing friends home and not mentioning their relative deprivation, and some talked of being isolated because children wouldn't play with them because they were poor:

> *It was in school and they said, one of my friends says 'I've got more money than you cos you're really, really poor, your family will always be poor' and it really upset me.*
> (Girl, eight years)

Conversely, children who had good friendships described them as being a protective influence against bullying and a buffer against the deprivations of poverty. One nine-year-old boy described how he didn't feel afraid of the gangs at school because he had good friends who would back him up. For another, however, aged 11, it was by joining a gang that he had achieved a sense of safety and belonging in the context of insecurity both at home and in the neighbourhood, as well as relief from the boredom of a life restricted by poverty. While he had a group who 'stuck up for each other' and had 'something to do' (largely getting into fights), he was clearly being drawn into a culture of violence and the risk of criminalisation.

PROFESSIONAL OR SEMI-PROFESSIONAL SUPPORT WORKERS

Professionals or voluntary support workers were sometimes included in children's support networks. A few children included one or more teachers (those who they particularly enjoyed being with at school) in their social network and a third of children said that, if they had a problem while at school (these were usually conflicts with peers or bullying rather than family issues), they would tell a teacher. Just one child included her social worker in her social network, although 55 per cent of the children had a social worker – a rather worrying finding, which suggests a lack of engagement by social workers with young children, for whatever reason (see Chapter 6). Two other children included support workers from local family support groups with whom they had developed close relationships.

POVERTY AND CHILDREN'S WELL-BEING – THE FIVE OUTCOMES

Children in poverty have by definition not achieved economic well-being in the present, as a result of their parents' access to income. Their ability to do so in the future may be affected by many of the other ways in which poverty affects their well-being, as well as by the impacts of parents' well-being on their parenting. The direct impacts identified in this study are summarised below in relation to the four outcomes other than economic well-being.

1. *Being healthy*

   - Poor housing conditions (including damp and draughts) and inability to afford costs of heating ⟶ asthma, respiratory conditions.

   - Overcrowding ⟶ greater conflict between siblings, lack of sleep.

   - Neighbourhood violence and crime ⟶ risks to safety, physical and mental health (especially deprived areas).

   - Worry about parental stress, excess responsibility for supporting parents ⟶ mental health risks, possible physical health effects.

   - Worry about parental and sibling ill-health, sibling conflicts and behaviour problems, vulnerability to bullying at school, direct stresses of poverty ⟶ mental health risks.

   - Domestic violence and ongoing fear after separation, neglect and physical abuse ⟶ mental health risks.

   - Inability to afford costs of counselling/therapy for children traumatised by, for example, sexual abuse, domestic violence, bereavement.

   - Poor diet (lack of food, lack of fresh food and reliance on cheap, processed, non-perishable foods) ⟶ risks of obesity, heart disease and short life expectancy.

   - Inability to afford necessary special diets ⟶ range of health problems and allergies.

   (Continued)

- Impact of lack of stimulating activities (parental mental health problems, costs) on cognitive and social and emotional development.

2. *Staying safe*

- Inability to afford alternative childcare ⟶ inadequate supervision (neglect), in some cases the context of sexual abuse.

- Poverty-related stress as part of context of physical abuse.

- Lack of options for respite from difficult parent–child relationships ⟶ increased parental stress and risk of physical abuse.

- Violence from siblings with behaviour problems, exacerbated by overcrowding, inability to afford different activities outside the house.

- Self-harm and risky behaviour as a result of unresolved distress (and lack of access to counselling/therapy).

- Bullying associated with poverty (especially affluent areas, possibly more violent including weapons in deprived areas).

3. *Enjoying and achieving*

- Impact of poverty-related bullying on participation.

- Impact of lack of sleep (related to overcrowding) on concentration.

- Barriers to full participation because of extra costs (e.g. school trips, buying a poppy on Poppy Day).

- Barriers to achievement because of hidden costs (e.g. lack of computers/internet access and need for homework).

- Exclusion as result of behaviour problems (often linked to unresolved trauma).

- Barriers to friendships because of lack of common experiences (both shared in school and apart out of school, including going to cinema, latest computer games, holidays).

- Lack of access to sports and leisure opportunities because of costs of activity, transport and hidden extras (especially affluent areas).

- Lack of safe play areas (especially deprived areas).

4. *Making a positive contribution*

- Risks of anti-social behaviour as a result of boredom; lack of access to alternative activities; opportunity to escape conflict and overcrowding at home, and to resist exclusion and gain protection against threats by belonging to local gangs (especially deprived areas).

REVISITING THE CYCLE OF DISADVANTAGE

Growing up in poverty increases the risk of living in poverty as an adult; the reasons for the persistence of poverty through the life cycle are not clear-cut but are likely to involve numerous interrelated forms of deprivation (Blandon and Gibbons, 2006). Many of the children in this study have to overcome not only the disadvantage of growing up in poverty but also numerous other difficulties, including children's and parents' mental and physical health problems, poor experiences of care from one or both parents, family traumas connected to maltreatment, domestic violence, bereavement, relationship breakdown and/or other events, child or sibling behavioural problems, bullying, and sometimes being surrounded by the threat and the culture of violence and crime. Important factors contributing to resilience were good experiences of care from parents (preferably both) and additional support from other family relationships, predominantly grandmothers. Of particular importance to good experiences and engagement in school were peer relationships, both with supportive 'best' friends and with interest-sharing friends, who protected children from vulnerability to bullying and some of the deprivations of growing up in poverty.

Parents were well aware of the disadvantages their children faced in growing up in poverty. However, only a few expressed the concern that their children would remain disadvantaged throughout their lives. Most parents expressed the belief or hope that their children would overcome the various disadvantages they faced, of which poverty was one, and achieve a more financially secure and happier life than their parents. Children largely shared this view in their aspirations and expectations of their futures, often talking about wanting to earn enough so they could give money to their parents and make their lives happier, and to work in professions that made life better for other people, including teachers, doctors and police. At the end of every child's interview, we asked them what they would like to be when they grew up. Their answers reveal their high aspirations at this stage in their lives and their belief that these opportunities are open to them:

What would you like to be when you grow up?

Something that's fun and that's worth a lot of money, I might like to put graphics into films for Disney or something like that.
(Girl, 11 years, affluent area)

A person that makes stuff and a newslady and dance band singer.
(Girl, six years, deprived area)

Car designer. Cos I love cars.
(Boy, nine years, deprived area)

A vet.
(Girl, 11 years, deprived area)

Either an astrophysicist or a paediatric [doctor] *working with kids.*
(Girl, ten years, affluent area)

A magician.
(Boy, nine years, deprived area)

Like a veterinary nurse, police officer or a doctor, or a professional, professional horse rider with like tons of horses, or one cool one.
(Girl, 11 years, affluent area)

A teacher ... I just always wanted to be a teacher.
(Girl, ten years, affluent area)

Probably a rocket scientist ... because I'm really into space and quite good at maths and stuff and I like going on computers or I might be, wanting to be a, a pilot or something or an astronaut or a footballer.
(Boy, nine years, affluent area)

Famous footballer.
(Boy, ten years, deprived area)

An ambulance driver.
(Girl, six years, deprived area)

I'd be a police officer ... So I can take naughty people away ... And lock them up in jail.
(Girl, five years, affluent area)

A find-out person ... Like you. [A researcher]
(Girl, seven years, deprived area)

To be a doctor.
(Boy, six years, deprived area)

A nurse.
(Girl, six years, deprived area)

I would like to be a doctor, a policewoman or just a normal worker. Because [a doctor would] *help people's lives and it would help them get better. Because* [a policewoman would] *see all the crime going on and to stop it all and help people not be naughty and things like that. Because* [as a shop worker] *you could earn money and probably give it away to charity or give it to Children in Need or people like that.*
(Girl, nine years, affluent area)

Sociologist or a lawyer ... or a footballer.
(Boy, 11 years, deprived area)

If children 'learn to be poor' and lower their aspirations accordingly, as there is much evidence to suggest (Shropshire and Middleton, 1999), most of the children in our study had not yet done so. They had, however, learnt that life was often unsafe and uncertain, and had already begun consciously to protect others (mainly their parents) from their needs and wishes. Such a response to their circumstances, if it becomes habitual, is unlikely to help them to fulfil their potential.

NOTES

1. Differences were tested using the Mann-Whitney test; $p<0.05$ for all significant differences discussed.

2. See Radford and Hester (2006) for full discussion of the courts' responses to contested child contact cases where there has been domestic violence.

3. Differences were tested using the Mann-Whitney test; $p<0.05$ for all significant differences discussed.

6 Experience of services – promoting social inclusion or intensifying exclusion?

KEY POINTS

- In all service contexts, the relationships that parents established with professionals were central to their experience of services. Parents valued people who listened to them, treated them with respect as equals, were sensitive to their circumstances and showed them care when they needed it. Continuity of such relationships was highly valued and loss of a trusted worker a key source of disappointment with services.

- Some experiences of services exacerbated stress, social exclusion and powerlessness, including:
  - long waits for repairs and rehousing from housing authorities, especially in the deprived areas
  - long waiting times from referral to first appointment for mental health professionals
  - high thresholds for intervention from social services.

- Services could also be a lifeline, recognising the difficulty of parents' situations and offering support, practical help or referral on to other agencies. In particular:
  - GPs were more commonly used for support than either social workers or health visitors, and were highly valued for knowing the parent and family well
  - health visitors were found reassuring in a fairly similar way, but appointments were not frequent or reliable enough
  - schools had sometimes worked hard to help children with behaviour problems or to respond flexibly to difficult situations of parents
  - counselling was found very helpful by many (though not all), especially if it was available long term
  - voluntary organisations were an important source of specialist help.

- Parents often found it very hard to ask for help, for a range of reasons. They also often lacked information about services available, as sometimes too did professionals. There were many other barriers to service use, including lack of free or affordable services being available (especially in affluent areas), childcare and transport costs, and the impacts of mental health problems on energy and motivation.

- In schools, communication was central to how parents experienced them. Inability to afford extras such as school trips meant children could be excluded from valuable opportunities, and some parents felt humiliated by this issue, especially in affluent areas. Parents easily felt intimidated in schools and found advocacy support very valuable when conflict arose. Schools in the deprived areas in particular were developing innovative ways of engaging parents living in poverty and parents from BME communities.

(Continued)

- Referrals and investigations over child protection concerns caused much fear and confusion for parents – insufficient care seemed sometimes to have been taken to allay these anxieties to enable parents to explain their circumstances fully so that decisions could be made on a fully informed basis.

- Parents whose children had behaviour problems had often found it very difficult to get help. Schools' responses had sometimes been punitive rather than helpful, making family situations worse. Social services had tended to regard the issue as low priority unless the child was directly at risk from the parent. The way social work concerns with children's safety were framed sometimes led to sibling abuse, parents' experience of victimisation by a child and children's self-harm being ignored.

- Recruitment and retention problems in social work, group practices for GPs and changing systems of health visitor allocation all potentially threaten the ability of parents to build a relationship with a practitioner who can get to know them, gain their confidence and help them to access further services.

- Professionals talked of both positive developments in and ongoing barriers to multi-agency working. A particular concern was that the emotional impact of the work could make effective work least likely with the most troubled families.

For the families in our study, contact with services could be a lifeline, relieving stress or at least helping them to manage it, and offering opportunities for healing, participation and social inclusion. It could also be a source of massive stress, frustration and disappointment, leaving people not only with unmet needs but also further excluded from participation in their communities and the opportunities open to others. People approach services with expectations influenced by their personal histories, current circumstances and knowledge of the service, and user views have to be interpreted with care and an appreciation of the service context and professional roles (this was one of the reasons we interviewed professionals as well as families). The experiences of both parents and professionals are drawn on in this chapter to identify ways in which services helped or hindered low-income families and the individuals within them.

It is organised by service, but a recurring theme across services was the importance of the way parents felt treated by individual practitioners and the relationships they established with them. Participants valued professionals who listened to them, were genuinely interested in them and gave time to them, showed them care, sensitivity and respect, offered appropriate support and information, and treated them as equals without judging or talking down to them. People who offered this could become, in attachment terms, 'a secure base', someone they could talk to about their concerns, the knowledge of which was reassuring often beyond the use actually made of them. The person a parent identified as someone they would go to about problems could be located in a wide range of different contexts – they included teachers, family support workers, GPs, social workers, health visitors, volunteers and voluntary sector workers, a probation officer and a community police officer. The importance of such relationships is often obscured in the language in which interventions are discussed and the terms in which solutions are framed, where organisational structure, legislation, technology and targets are more common concerns.

The significance of relationships with professionals is likely to be greater for families and individuals who are socially isolated – in our study, 28 per cent named professionals among the people they relied most on for support, and one of the major sources of disappointment in services was when a worker the parent or child had come to trust left. While workers will of course leave, more attention is needed in all contexts both to the handling of endings and to the ways in which organisational structures, the status of professions and other factors such as pay and opportunities for career progression may affect the potential for trusted relationships to be established for people with high levels of trauma and insecurity in their backgrounds. The fear and hatred of dependency that permeates current policy, despite growing recognition of interdependency as the condition of humanity and relationships as essential to well-being (Hoggett, 2000; Cooper and Lousada, 2005), inhibit attention to such issues.

HOUSING – *LIKE BATTING YOUR HEAD AGAINST A BRICK WALL*

The stress caused to parents by poor housing and the impact on children's well-being have been described in previous chapters. To recap briefly, many homes were overcrowded, conditions were often appalling and environments sometimes unsafe, especially in the deprived areas. An additional source of stress, however, was dealing with housing authorities, since the majority of families were dependent on social housing. Parents talked of long waits for repairs, even when radiators were leaking and they had no heating, and despite problems being reported repeatedly to the council. There were even longer waits for rehousing. Some had been waiting in temporary or unsuitable accommodation for several years. One had succeeded in being rehoused only after 11 years, despite having a child psychologist, social worker and solicitor all fighting on her behalf. Parents' attempts to influence housing authorities included repeated (and costly) phone calls, writing to their councillor, seeking letters of support from doctors, school heads, health visitors, social workers and (for one) taking the local authority to court. '*Nothing happens*' was a recurring phrase in describing the effect of such strategies, although one who had had to live with her parents (who had abused her as a child) had eventually won a tribunal case and was rehoused. Most were left feeling there was no effective help available and some were pushed to desperate measures in the attempt to generate it (claiming their parenting was affected more than it was or asking a charity to say they were evicting the family when they weren't).

Housing authorities (HAs) no doubt used any rule available to deflect demands on overstretched resources, in the context of very limited housing stock and a drastically reduced role in social housing. In doing so, however, they often appeared dismissive of the claims and insensitive to the needs of their tenants. A woman who had left a violent partner and returned to live with her mother was told she had made herself 'intentionally homeless' and waited several years to get rehoused again. Another whose flat was damaged when the flat upstairs flooded was told to claim on her neighbour's insurance, as the upstairs flat was privately owned – she didn't know how to do this so got nothing. The bidding system, under which those on the housing list have to bid for specific properties to be considered and the property is allocated to the applicant with highest priority (and people therefore bid numerous times with no result), caused huge frustration and the process was described as 'endless'. One parent, who had been told to 'wait and keep bidding', had also been warned not to bring a letter from a doctor as it wouldn't make a difference, although her child suffered from asthma, which was affected by the cold.

When councils had disputed their responsibility – for fixing a broken door or rehousing a family – occasionally parents had won. One woman going through a divorce had been told by the council that they had no responsibility as she was still the co-owner of a house. She looked up the relevant law in the library, found that the council should offer her temporary housing, got herself a solicitor and won her case. A man described being told by the council that they had to remove a window because of building regulations. He had asked to see the regulations and found they couldn't produce any so the window stayed. But to fight such battles successfully requires resources that many families did not have and most, especially those in the deprived areas, felt both hugely stressed by the effort required (one described trying to get rehoused as 'like a full-time job') and powerless to influence this most basic issue, their home circumstances. We did not interview housing workers but, from comments made spontaneously in the focus groups, even professionals in the deprived areas were made helpless by their encounters with the housing department. As one health visitor put it:

> *It gets to the point where you just think what's the point? If someone mentions housing to you, you just think what's the point?*

In the affluent areas, housing conditions were generally better, and progressive and supportive housing associations were mentioned by professionals. Although housing authorities were similarly unresponsive over repairs and rehousing, the parents we interviewed mostly had more personal or financial resources to manage this, either by standing up to the council (as in the cases described in the previous paragraph) or by finding a way to pay for repairs themselves. Whether this was due to the sharp elbows of a middle-class background or location, a greater sense of entitlement seemed reflected in outrage at what was felt to be degrading and disrespectful treatment from housing authorities. This was expressed by those from both middle- and working-class backgrounds in the affluent area. One man who defined his background as working class was trying to get the council to repair his front door but felt he had been fobbed off for over a year by workers who denied there was anything wrong:

> *Well you're claiming benefit and you're living in a council house and all this so they think well they think you're thick for a start off, they think you're stupid.*

CASE EXTRACT

R: *The radiators were very old fashioned, they were very old fashioned, they leaked. Once I decorated my place became a wreck again when they leaked in the house. They caused damage to carpets and what have you. I called the council, they couldn't be ... they didn't turn up to do anything for ages and ages, you know. I had to get H [a voluntary organisation specialising in housing advice] involved where they were going to help me to get financially settled with this matter. Because obviously it all came out of my pocket to have the repairs done and all that. Anyway that never worked out the first time I went to H. I was very upset with those people.*

(Continued)

> I: *Was you?*
>
> R: *Because I ended up in hospital again. Because I was so stressed with having to deal with it all. You know thinking that I had some help, outside help. And when it came down to the crunch they weren't helping me. You know. But this time round I've been satisfied. Yeah I've been very satisfied.*

SCHOOLS – *GOOD COMMUNICATION MAKES ALL THE DIFFERENCE*

Parents in both deprived and affluent areas had had mixed experiences with schools. Where teachers had time for them, took an interest in their children, were friendly and approachable, informed them when the school had a concern about their children and took them seriously when they did, they were by and large happy with their schools, especially (but not only) if their children were also doing well. Some had found schools particularly helpful in responding flexibly to difficult circumstances, for example when a lone mother was in hospital and her oldest son had to drop a younger child to school early in order to get to work on time himself and a teacher had come in early to be with him. Where communication was poor and classes or schools were too big and busy to notice what was going on for their children, arrangements made were not always kept, or parents felt looked down on or their circumstances not recognised, they were less happy.

The experience of feeling disrespected was sometimes related to low income, primarily in the affluent areas where poverty was a less familiar issue to schools. One parent described feeling humiliated by having to reply saying he couldn't afford it every time the school's standard letter asking for a contribution to trips came round, despite having explained his situation to the school. Another felt intimidated when she was asked for a contribution of £7.25 within four days of the letter for a trip. She ticked the no box and, when the head asked to see her and told her what the money was for, she eventually agreed to pay £3.25. Disrespect was also experienced in relation to other differences, however – differences, that is, from institutions that were perceived primarily as white and middle-class. A mother with a daughter of mixed race felt one school had made assumptions about her background (that she was a lone parent) that led to discrimination – she had not felt taken seriously but when her partner (who was white and middle-class) got in touch the response was quite different. Schools can seem very intimidating places to parents, with their parenting under scrutiny from teachers echoing the way their own school work was in childhood. The support of another professional or support worker 'on their side' helped some to speak and feel listened to in meetings.

Parents' concerns included choice/allocation of school, standards, the costs of equipping children for school, and the school's response to behaviour problems and special needs, bullying, truancy and child protection concerns (in relation to all of which issues how the school communicated with parents over them was a key theme). Cost issues included school uniforms, school trips and bus fares. Grants for school uniforms did not always cover the full cost and one parent suggested schools should sell their logo so that parents could buy cheaper clothes and sew it on. Trips were discussed also by teachers and there is clearly a dilemma for schools over wanting to offer what may be particularly valuable extra experience for children whose lives are restricted by poverty, and not wanting to put pressure on parents who cannot afford trips or do not want to subject their children to the demeaning and divisive experience of being left out. One teacher had been surprised recently when a trip had been announced and the children had looked anxious until they had been told it was free, as she had not realised how aware the children were of the constraints on their parents. Another commented that it is the children of the working poor who lose out most since, where subsidies exist, they tend to go to those children whose families are on income support. Bus fares were a problem for those who lived just closer than the limit for assistance (two miles for children under eight years and three miles for those over), or who were moved between temporary housing and tried to maintain continuity of schooling for their children despite greater distance.

Schools can play an important role in relation to child protection, but their training and experience of dealing with cases varies widely (Baginsky, 2003, 2006). Social workers in the deprived areas tended to regard local schools as more experienced, having had many of their children on the Child Protection Register (CPR), than did social workers in the affluent areas where schools' responses were perceived as improving but still variable. Despite this, parents who discussed these issues (only four in total) reported more positive experience in the affluent areas. This may have been partly due to the circumstances of the cases – both of those in the affluent area involved domestic violence (in one the children had told the school nurse, in the other the school coordinator for child protection cases had become involved after the children were put on the CPR because of emotional abuse from the father) and these people had provided important support for both mother and children over some time.

In the two cases in the deprived areas, the school had informed social services[1] of their concerns without informing the mother first – in both cases, the case was closed fairly quickly, but both mothers were angered by the failure of the school to communicate with them direct, in circumstances where they had an established relationship with the school over other concerns (the child's disability in one case, behaviour problems in the other). It may also be that, for schools with many child protection issues, familiarity combined with overload may sometimes result in lack of care to consider how best to handle each case. Judgements about when to discuss referrals with parents before making them, or when doing so may themselves place the child at risk, are not of course easy and teachers may prefer to be overcautious, especially where pressed for time and anxious. They may also be asked by child protection teams not to inform parents for fear that parents will put pressure on and silence their children, leaving the teachers in a difficult position in terms of maintaining their own relationships with parents.

By far the most common concern in relation to schools among the parents we interviewed was schools' responses to children with behaviour problems. Several had struggled to have the nature of their children's problems recognised and this had sometimes taken a considerable time, even years. Some children had been excluded for bad behaviour, sometimes repeatedly, when their mothers felt that their behaviour problems had their roots in previous abuse, neglect or traumatic loss/separation, or were associated with disability (especially autism) and their children needed help.

CASE EXTRACT

One parent felt her son's behaviour problems were linked to a recent diagnosis she had been given of a brain tumour:

... he can't talk to me about the things he wants to say. 'Well, are you gonna die mum?', he can't say that to me, he doesn't even wanna think it you know, so back here in the primary school ... there should have been people prepared to take time out, put school work second for a change ... You know 'Let's find out what your issue is, what's going on ...' 'Well fuckin 'ell my mum's got a fuckin brain tumour I'm angry about it'. It wasn't, no it wasn't so, when Richard got into fights at school, Laurence would take on them fights and in my head that's his relief that's his emotions coming out.

Not only did this fail to help but it could also make family situations worse. One mother had found it very hard to explain to an autistic child why he had been excluded and felt he had blamed her, which she had found extremely distressing. Another child had truanted and the mother had been fined £120, apparently without any attempt to find out why the child had been missing school (she had been bullied). Another child had been referred by his school to social services for behaviour problems, on the assumption that these were related to parenting problems. This had caused considerable stress and anxiety for the parents, but the child had later been diagnosed with ADHD, although there were clearly parenting problems too.

Once a problem had been recognised and labelled as a special need (rather than punished as naughtiness or bad behaviour), there had been a range of responses, some of which parents had found helpful, some less so. Some children had been sent to special schools or referral units and, although some parents had felt less stigmatised themselves in this context, and reassured by staff who were familiar with the issues and could support them and their children, others (and on occasion the same parent) had worried that their children were influenced for the worse by the behaviour of other pupils, the stigma of exclusion from mainstream schools or lower educational standards.

Many other forms of help were offered by schools and much appreciated by parents – including referrals to a range of services and professionals as appropriate to the needs of the child and of the family (including child psychologists and educational psychologists, home tutors, mentors who could involve the child in activities outside school, part-time exclusion centres and boarding schools, parenting courses and family support workers), or simply giving tips for parents on managing behaviour (e.g. behaviour charts with rewards). Some parents felt some schools had really worked hard to help their children, though what worked varied for different children and sometimes it felt like nothing did. Schools could also sometimes make what seemed excessive demands on parents, e.g. that a child be taken home for lunch, local education authority (LEA) allocation policy could undermine hard-won progress, e.g. where the family was rehoused and the child had to move school, and some schools were clearly more reluctant than others to include and manage children with behaviour problems.

Teachers we interviewed also discussed provision for children with special needs as an issue of particular relevance to low-income families. A learning support unit for children with behaviour problems in one of the deprived-area schools was reported to have been welcomed by most parents, offering them opportunities to offload and much needed help, with only occasional parental resistance – this was a school with a relatively low level of behaviour problems and good communication both internally and externally. Nurture groups run by speech therapists were being developed in the affluent areas where there was growing concern at the number of children, mostly from low-income families, coming to school with poorly developed language ability, attributed to lack of stimulation and interaction at home.

Other issues discussed by teachers included trips/extra costs (discussed above), engaging children in education and involving parents. Teachers in both areas were conscious of the disadvantages children from low-income families brought with them to school and the opportunities schools had to make a difference to their lives. Positive developments included homework clubs (so that children whose parents lacked the confidence or capacity to help them with their homework could get help elsewhere), the use of the personal, social, health and citizenship education (PSHCE) curriculum to address issues such as budgeting, diet, and drugs, and the use of school councils to encourage children to find and express their voices. Teachers also talked of the need for constant awareness of the restrictions that poverty imposed on some children's lives, so that they did not unwittingly exclude or alienate children by assuming, for example, that all those in a class had been to the cinema or to a zoo. Constraints on their ability to counter the impacts of poverty and social exclusion included the loss of space for play-based learning with the extension of the formal curriculum (to the particular disadvantage of those children with limited opportunities at home), lack of discretion to make the content of the curriculum relevant and engaging (in the affluent areas, teachers complained of having to teach German to children without adequate skills in English), classes too large to give children sufficient individual attention and the tendency of children not to mix much across income differences (because of the effects of costs, partly on school experiences but partly also on friendships outside school).

Although parents we interviewed placed a high value on communication with schools, teachers, especially in the affluent areas, talked of the difficulties of involving parents. To an extent it seemed that parents who were already struggling with the demands of parenting and living in poverty appreciated the involvement of schools when it assisted them with, or relieved them of, some of their responsibilities but not when it increased them. Teachers in the deprived areas talked of parents wanting teachers to do things they felt unable to do effectively themselves (e.g. telling children to read) and of being grateful that their children were looked after at school – both of which may apply to all parents, of course. Teachers in the affluent areas reported that it was 'impossible' to get parents from poorer areas involved in parent–teacher associations (PTAs) and often difficult to get them to come to parents' evenings. While the reasons floated for lack of parental involvement – feeling intimidated both by the school and by middle-class parents, lack of confidence in such environments, lack of motivation or aspiration – may all be relevant, the nature and meaning of involvement needs also to be questioned and the context of parents' lives kept in mind if the judging of poor parents against a standard based on middle-class lifestyles (i.e. 'othering') is to be avoided.

Some schools in deprived areas had developed other ways of engaging parents than PTAs and parents' evenings, e.g. a parents' coffee morning. Teachers here emphasised the need to be informal, accessible and flexible, e.g. having a coffee morning without coffee and biscuits during Ramadan! A dedicated facilitator to drive such initiatives and make personal contact with parents, learning mentors for children who could also engage parents on a one-to-one basis and careful timing of meetings (e.g. first thing in the morning – 'we don't let them leave the gates!') were recommended.

HEALTH AND SOCIAL CARE

Parents in our study were asked which professionals they received support from and to indicate who they would go to for support around personal worries and worries about their children. More women than men used professionals for such support and GPs were more commonly used for both types of support than either health visitors or social workers. Figure 6.1 shows the proportions across the sample as a whole.

Figure 6.1: Parents seeking help from different professionals for personal or child issues

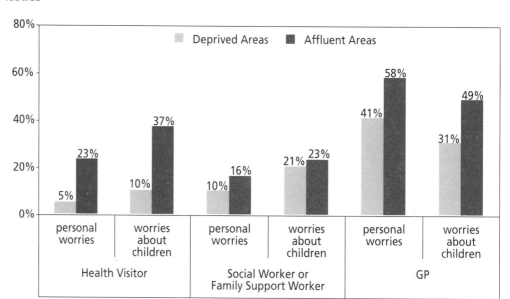

More parents of course *had* GPs than had social workers, so the difference is partly due to availability (though none the less important for that) but, of those families in contact with social services, there were still more who included their GP as giving support around personal worries than their social worker/family support worker (SW/FSW), and GPs remained a significant source of support for worries about children. BME parents in London (both Bangladeshi and black) were more likely than white parents to talk to GPs about personal worries. White parents in the affluent contexts were also more than twice as likely to do so than white parents in London. Whether these differences reflect the availability of other sources of support, different perceptions of services or actual differences in services is unknown, and would require further research. Health visitors were also used more for support with worries about children than were SW/FSWs, especially in the affluent areas.

Barriers to take-up of services are discussed first in this section, then the parents' experience of these three professional groups and of other health professionals.

BARRIERS TO SERVICE USE – *YOU REALLY HAVE TO FIGHT TO GET ANY HELP*

Many parents found it extremely difficult to ask for and get the help they needed. Some of the barriers were largely internal. Shame at admitting to not coping or reluctance to face up to problems that carry a stigma, especially in relation to mental health problems or difficulties with parenting, could inhibit people, as could pride in coping without help or loyalty (e.g. to an abusive partner or parent). For some, self-image was a barrier, since they saw themselves as not the kind of person who uses certain kinds of service, such as social services departments (SSDs) or lone parent organisations, or who uses any service for certain kinds of things, such as help with parenting. Lack of energy to break out of a habit of isolation (particularly if depressed) and/or fear, sometimes related to past experiences with a particular kind of organisation, e.g. being taken into care themselves as a child, could also inhibit access to services, as could the value attributed to privacy and self-reliance, which may have defensive and/or cultural dimensions.

Other barriers were more external, related to availability, perception and experience of services, though there may clearly be an interaction, e.g. where a bad experience of a service leaves the person reluctant to seek help again. There were language barriers for some, including where interpreters were available but did not always convey accurately what was meant. Services that required continual chasing to get a response, or that raised people's expectations and then let them down (most commonly when a trusted worker left and they could not face starting again), were offputting. Relevant services were sometimes not available (especially in the affluent areas where services for low-income families were rare) or appeared to exclude the parent. One woman had been told she could not use a service for Asian women as she was Indian not Bangladeshi and some services were perceived as for women even if they were open to men too. Direct costs, transport costs and childcare problems were also barriers to service use.

Some parents lacked information, not knowing of services that were available. Professionals too, especially in the deprived areas where initiatives had proliferated at a rapid rate, found it difficult to keep up to date with what was available, though they were also sometimes frustrated by knowing that services they were aware of had long waiting lists. There is a need for local information to be easily available to parents and professionals, and to be kept up-to-date, and for services available to be sufficiently resourced to meet need. There is also a need for publicity campaigns to encourage parents to seek help, offering models for doing so that parents from different backgrounds and in a range of situations could identify with (similar perhaps to the Zero Tolerance campaign on domestic violence), if the preventive aims of current policy are to be met.

GPs – *SOMEONE WHO KNOWS YOU*

There were many very positive comments about GPs, largely framed in terms of someone who knew the parent and family well, who parents could talk to and who they felt would listen to what they had to say.

CASE QUOTES

[When my GP] senses I need help, she will. She knows a lot of what's gone, gone on and she seems to remember it actually and remember a lot of it. She's quite supportive.
(Lone mother who suffered depression linked to domestic violence, which went on after separation and a very stressful struggle to reclaim tax credits that had been wrongly deducted from her)

I found my own doctors and my own health visitor, because they know me, very good. I found social services, I don't think they took it seriously enough.
(Lone mother whose ex-husband had been violent to her and the children, and who was seeking shared residence of the children even though his son was terrified of him)

[My GP is] very good, very good. He's very good yeah, he knows me for a long time and he's able to feed back on my health and you know let me know what is important.
(Lone mother who suffers from schizophrenia and has been in and out of hospital many times)

The importance of GPs for support seemed partly due to the fact that they were seen regularly for other reasons – for medication for either a parent (e.g. anti-depressants, methadone) or for a child (e.g. Ritalin), for check-ups in relation to other medical conditions (e.g. diabetes) and consultation over child health concerns – and partly due to the trust and familiarity developed through confidentiality and continuity over time. The implications of changing organisational structures, such as group practices, for GPs' ability to get to know their patients well, and for patients' ability to see the person they trust (which may require some confidence and skill in using the appointment system) is thus a matter of concern, and was raised by health visitors who were interviewed. Parents mostly still had a single named GP, but one who was registered with a group practice said she could talk to some of the doctors but not all. She felt some didn't want to listen and she had clearly withdrawn from contact as a result, saying she was keeping her worries bottled up until she saw her health visitor. Fears about information being shared more freely in a group practice may also undermine trust.

GPs had offered valuable practical help through referring parents or children to other professionals or services (psychologists, child psychologists, psychiatrists, counsellors, voluntary organisations and, on one occasion, a self-help group), signing them off work (including for one when a smoky work atmosphere posed a threat to her pregnancy) and writing letters in their support (e.g. for an application for rehousing). Referrals included one made to social services over child protection concerns – the GP had been very supportive to the parent, explaining the process and listening and acknowledging her perspective, so trust had been maintained – the parent still said she would talk to her GP first if she had any problem with parenting. Many parents had been prescribed anti-depressants and several had accepted the prescription but not taken them, either because they preferred to manage in their own way or because of side-effects.

Negative experiences included GPs too busy to take time to listen, slow recognition of the seriousness of mental health problems or response to the need for a referral, and insufficient recognition of their circumstances (one woman had tried to get a doctor to come out for an emergency visit, on the advice of NHS Direct, when her daughter had been vomiting blood and had been told to take a taxi and come in, with both a sick daughter and a toddler in tow). Advice given was not always found helpful (another woman had consulted her GP when at the end of her tether over her son's behaviour problems and had apparently been told to write everything down and drink hot milk before she went to bed), and nor were referrals (another felt pathologised and labelled when she sought advice on exercises to get her belly into shape and was referred for help with body image issues). Referrals made were also often followed, through no fault of the GPs of course, by long waiting lists to see GP counsellors, psychologists and psychiatrists.

HEALTH VISITORS – *NICE BUT NOT OFTEN ENOUGH* Although all parents should see a health visitor at least once after the birth of a baby, only 87 per cent of parents in the affluent areas and 43 per cent in the deprived areas reported having seen a health visitor (although it is possible that more may have done so but may not have identified correctly or remembered the role of the worker they saw). Ghate and Hazel (2002) similarly found apparent gaps in coverage – 32 per cent of low-income parents in their sample had never been in contact with a health visitor and 17 per cent of those with pre-school children.[2] The difference between areas was greater for use of health visitors than for any other professional, which may reflect a lack of resources to meet need and therefore a more targeted service in deprived areas, although some of those parents who had not seen a health visitor may also have been missed because of recent immigration. One who had arrived in the country when her son was eight months old had asked for a health visitor but had never heard back from the GP she registered with. Some of those who had seen a health visitor had had home visits, others had been seen only at a clinic. Some had seen their health visitor only once, others more frequently.

Health visitors were valued for support and reassurance for the parent, advice and information relating to children and referrals to, information about or advocacy with other services. Positive comments were often framed fairly similarly to those about GPs – in terms of the health visitor being someone who knew the mother and who she could talk to. One woman particularly appreciated her health visitor taking her aside whenever she visited the surgery to check she was OK when she was depressed. This kind of spontaneous contact without an appointment was something health visitors feared losing with changing structures (see below). Negative experiences included being treated in a rude and patronising way and not being given information about other services, but the most common negative comment concerned the infrequency or unreliability of appointments – these comments could be summed up as 'nice but not often enough'.

As still (just) a universal and hence non-stigmatised service, with home visiting and/or easy access often in GP surgeries, health visitors are in a unique position to support families with young children and signpost or refer them on to other services – as one of those interviewed put it, they '*can set kids up for life … we're the only people, nought to three*'. Staff retention is also relatively good, or has been, although some of the health visitors we talked to said it was declining as a result of the demands of the transition to geographical working and primary care trust (PCT) budget restrictions on recruitment. As such it has received surprisingly little recognition in recent policy, although the aim of identifying families at risk earlier has recently brought the role of health visitors and midwives back into focus (HM Government, 2006a). As a new high-profile initiative to offer parenting experts to deprived areas is launched (discussed in Chapter 4), it is worth a reminder that there already is a service offering help with parenting, which is overstretched and under-resourced.

Health visitors interviewed described a number of ways they helped low-income families, in addition to those already noted – giving practical help over budgeting or working out shift patterns to allow time for family life as well as work, running drop-ins or groups that offer mothers opportunities for social contact and mutual support with others, or simply recognising that life sounded tough for mothers on low incomes. Some clinics now had a CAB worker coming in to offer benefit advice, a service that was clearly valuable and worth extending. Some cost-saving developments, such as the use of nursery nurses as lower qualified and cheaper staff who were less threatening to parents to do some of the work health visitors used to do, were welcomed. The extension of their role to work with older children was also cautiously welcomed since they were often consulted anyway about older children by families they had known for years and were in contact with for younger children, although some fears were expressed about dilution of expertise, and the need for extra training to enable them to help parents of children with behaviour problems was identified.

However, they expressed huge frustration at the impact of resource constraints on the service they could provide and a concern that the service was being spread thinner and thinner. Lack of funding affected the core service but also meant extra services they wanted to provide, including those for vulnerable parents, could not be offered, or only (in one case) through the health visitor paying for the costs of publicity out of their own pocket. On a broader level it meant there were often too few services to refer parents to when a need was identified.

Health visitors also expressed concern at the possible impact of changes to the structure of the service on low-income families and on their ability to protect children at risk of maltreatment. Some welcomed the opportunities that geographical working (the attachment of health visitors to areas rather than GP practices) and corporate caseloads (the pooling of cases and allocation according to need) brought for team-working and for flexible and equitable use of resources, but were finding the process of transition challenging. Others expressed concerns about losing the direct relationship they currently have with GPs and the informal contact with families often associated with it. They were also worried that the fragmentation of the service, and an increased reliance on groupwork at clinics, schools or children's centres rather than home visiting, would interfere with the continuity that enables them to get to know families. They feared that the combined effect of these changes might result in families without strong communication skills or much confidence, and/or who were less well known to or more able to avoid professionals, getting lost in a more complex system and communication between health visitors and GPs being undermined.

OTHER HEALTH PROFESSIONALS – *WAY TOO LONG TO WAIT (ESPECIALLY FOR CHILDREN)*

A range of other health professionals had been seen by parents on their own or their children's behalf, including psychiatrists, psychologists, community psychiatric nurses, counsellors, speech therapists and CAMHS. Many of these experiences were positive in terms either of reassurance to parents about their parenting or more specialist help for specific issues. A number of issues were raised, however.

First, waiting times were often far too long from when referrals were made to first appointment – a mother whose ten-year-old daughter had witnessed domestic violence since birth and been sexually abused by her mother's partner for four years (the mother had also attempted suicide several times) had asked for counselling for the child and was still waiting six months later. Another woman, referred to a psychologist after disclosing two experiences of rape, one by a gang, the other by her uncle, who had had a child as a result, had to wait for two years for an initial appointment. Children as well as parents suffer from such delays.

Second, there was sometimes simply no free or affordable service available, especially for mental health problems such as depression or anxiety, or, if it was available, it was too short-term. One woman described a recent breakthrough after three or four years of counselling, but long-term, open-ended counselling of this kind was rare.

Third, appointment times were sometimes offered that were not possible for parents, e.g. clashing with the time children had to be picked up from school, and failing to meet the appointment offered meant another long wait. It should not be impossible for services to check on such commitments when a referral is first accepted.

Fourth, counselling was not a panacea for all. While many found it very helpful, children sometimes did not want to talk to a counsellor (though they perhaps might at a later date), and several parents were put off by their counsellor's approach, especially where the counsellor seemed to have an agenda of their own that was different from the parent's. One father also reported being unused to talking about emotions, though after a struggle he had found it helpful to open up.

Other issues raised, including frequent changes of worker (for speech therapy), lack of follow-up (from a community psychiatric nurse (CPN) and CAMHS), lack of understanding of children's behaviour problems and judgemental attitudes to parents, were reiterated in accounts of social workers and are discussed further in the next section.

SOCIAL WORKERS – YOU HAVE TO HIT YOUR CHILD TO GET ANY HELP

The social control role of social services (now children's services) departments in relation to parenting makes it unsurprising that parents' experiences of social workers were often mixed. Some parents had referred themselves, for help with their housing or financial situation, with a violent partner or ex-partner, with a child's behaviour problems or disability, or just when they felt unable to cope. More often in our sample they had been referred by others – neighbours, relatives and ex-partners (sometimes maliciously, using SSD involvement as a weapon in an ongoing war), and schools, GPs, hospitals and health visitors with concerns about their child's safety.

Where referrals were made by others, parents sometimes knew nothing until a social worker and police officer arrived unannounced on their doorsteps. In such circumstances, and even sometimes with warning, parents were often frightened, angry and confused during the investigation. The emotional impacts of investigation on parents have been noted in previous research, but they cannot be emphasised enough, as failure to appreciate, make space for and contain them can have highly damaging consequences. One woman who was suffering from post-natal depression after becoming pregnant from rape had told her GP of dropping her baby and he had referred the case to social services with her knowledge. In describing the subsequent investigation, she spoke of being asked by social workers why she had not terminated the pregnancy and then of apparently being told that they would take the baby if she didn't 'give them the answers' to their questions. Whether she remembered the conversation accurately or not, and her memory may have been affected (as no doubt was the encounter) by trauma, fear and confusion, and language problems, it is clear that she was unable to tell social workers the whole story behind her situation. As a result the outcome was that she was allowed to keep the baby so long as she was living with her aunt and uncle who could supervise. Her uncle was one of the men who had raped her, and it was a year before she sought help again, after renewed aggression from her uncle and her own attempted suicide.

Parents became involved with social services for a range of reasons: when a child was accused of abuse, when a child was abused or suspected of being abused by someone outside the family, when there were concerns about one or other partner's parenting causing risks to a child, when a child was disabled or seriously ill, or when a child had behaviour problems (situations could fall into more than one of these categories, of course). Parents whose children were disabled or ill, or had been abused by someone outside the family, had predominantly positive experiences and felt supported, except where there was a dispute over the cause of the child's problems (in one case where a child was thought by social workers to be neglected but was later found to be suffering from a developmental problem, and in another where the mother believed damage to a child's anus had been deliberately inflicted by the new partner of her children's father and social services accepted the partner's account that it was accidental). Parents involved because of concerns about their own or their partner's parenting had more mixed experiences (and sometimes one parent's was positive, the other's not), but some also felt that, despite fears to start with, the overall experience was positive, especially if they accepted the reason for intervention, developed a good relationship with the social worker within which they got support and reassurance alongside monitoring of their parenting, and had accessed practical help (e.g. help with childcare, debt, activities for children, day trips, parenting classes, support workers and other support services).

The most consistently negative comments, however, were from those parents who were involved with social services over children with behaviour problems. Again, a few had positive experiences here, where help from other services was forthcoming alongside support from the social worker. But most had sought help, often repeatedly, without success before any action was taken (as had one in the previous group, when he felt he was not coping). These parents had felt their difficulties in parenting their children were not taken seriously and were either dismissed, e.g. as just 'terrible twos', or were regarded as too low priority to justify help.

In six cases, only when they hit the child, threatened to abandon or kill him, or when he was sexually abused by someone else was action taken. These parents were frustrated and angry. One felt her son would not have been sexually abused if she had been listened to earlier when she had expressed fears that something was going to happen to her son, as she felt he was unable to understand risks and boundaries. Another parent had twice attacked social workers, as well as finally hitting her son in front of them, in her frustration at their response that, despite his violence to her, since she wasn't hurting him, they could do nothing. Another, who had finally been assessed after hitting her son, was nevertheless still waiting for help after an assessment that she felt was taking far too long, and she described social services as 'useless'. A man (in the previous group), who had not had concerns over children's behaviour problems but had been struggling as a lone father, described a similar sense of frustration and injustice after he had sought help for years and been offered nothing but reassurance that he was coping fine (when he felt he was not). Then he had suddenly received lots of intervention when he had hit his son's leg and the bruise had been noticed at school. This had been followed by another long wait before any effective help had been forthcoming. Some of these responses are no doubt the effect of limited resources, and all the professionals interviewed were aware of SSDs as 'very overstretched and underfunded', with the result that only families at crisis point would get help. However, it is also the result of the way priorities and concerns are framed, and this and other issues that contributed to poor experiences of SSDs are discussed below.

First, the way issues are framed sometimes conflicts with the reality of family life as parents (and children) experience it. While recognition of the risks parents may pose to children has been hugely important and children's welfare is rightly the paramount consideration, an exclusive focus on unidirectional harm (even complemented as it often is now by recognition of domestic violence as a common context) fits uneasily with the experience of those parents whose children, for whatever reason, are violent or abusive to them or their siblings.

It also sometimes seemed the case that only one child at a time entered the frame. So, for example, one mother whose oldest son had serious behaviour problems (including violence) was advised to kick him out of the house when he was 16 and help was withdrawn, but also asked by her social worker to help him out by feeding him sometimes. She did so, but his continued presence in the house clearly put her other children at risk and she struggled to manage this. The parent-to-child harm frame could also lead to dismissal of the needs of children whose distress was expressed through self-harm – one parent described professionals noticing her son's bruises, but losing interest as soon as they were accepted as self-inflicted. Managing to maintain the whole family in perspective, recognise the conflicting interests and needs within it, and negotiate the care and/or control role in relation to its different members is a complex but necessary task. Sometimes a problem that did seem a straightforward case of one parent harming a child (e.g. when a separated father, with a history of domestic violence, hit his children on a visit) was met with a response that seemed to obscure this to the rest of the family – the social worker decided to avoid the child protection route and simply recommended the mother got an injunction to keep the father out of the house. She felt this left all the responsibility to her and the child felt not taken seriously – she had wanted him 'told off'.

A further concern in terms of how issues are framed is the use of language. Two parents were upset when a relative (brother in one case, son in another) was described as a 'paedophile' or 'perpetrator' after incidents of sexual abuse – for the people with lifelong relationships with these individuals, they were clearly much more than what they were reduced to by these labels.

Second, communication was a crucial issue, with parents often feeling they were not listened to or taken seriously, and sometimes unclear about the nature of concerns or the meaning of interventions (especially when a child was placed on the CPR). Good communication is clearly more likely to occur in the context of a good working relationship (this was described in terms of someone you could talk to, who really listened, who took account of your feelings, who didn't talk down to you or stereotype you as a bad parent). It is not always easy to achieve in the context of child protection concerns.

Fear and confusion may get in the way of parents taking in information they are given. Social workers' agendas and the timing of interventions to prioritise children's needs necessarily conflict fairly often with parents' agendas, and insecure, frightened and resistant parents may be ill-equipped to manage hearing judgements that necessarily change over time. Lack of interpreters obviously inhibits communication. Staff turnover also undermines the ability to build the relationships in which effective communication can take place. Several parents described having a series of social workers, and the difficulty of starting again when one left – one family had had eight in three years, and the children's experience of being repeatedly let down as soon as they began to get to know a worker had resulted in them refusing to speak to the present one. Not everyone found change equally difficult but, even where it was relatively unproblematic, there was a transition time before the parent felt she knew a new worker well enough to talk to her.

A further barrier to communication may also be the increased reliance on risk factors in assessment – one parent, when asked how social services could improve, commented *'To listen to people more and really take in their feelings and that, you know. Because they don't, they just tick boxes, you know, and categorise you'*. Others felt judged by comments that either reflected normative assumptions (for example, for a man, questions about why he was not employed when he was unable to get a job) or an apparently crude use of risk factors (for example, a woman whose son's suspected sexual abuse was linked to her own experience of being sexually abused by her stepfather in childhood). In the latter case, the concern may well have been that the child had had contact with the same man, but sufficient care did not seem to have been taken to avoid reinforcing guilt and self-blame for her.

Third, there were issues about the nature and extent of help. Many forms of intervention were appreciated – help with claiming benefits, applying for grants and other financial problems, subsidised childcare or nursery places, parenting classes, outreach, family support workers or other workers who offered home visits and/or one-to-one time, contact with other families in family centres, holiday playschemes, residential holidays and other activities for children, support with rehousing or injunctions, and referrals for specialist help or to groups for mutual support. Very simple things, just reassurance or positive feedback, could be hugely important and, to some parents, social workers were literally a lifesaver.

But there was also much dissatisfaction with the long struggle it took to get any help at all for many (with repeated requests, long assessments and further long waits for referrals to become an actual service common), with the far too short-term nature of the help then offered and with some failures to follow through at all on actions agreed (effectively being apparently forgotten or dropped). One mother, whose son was referred for his violent behaviour to a psychologist who saw him twice then had a 'nervous breakdown', heard nothing more and was left thinking her son was just too difficult for anyone. Those who had been assessed were sometimes reassured and vindicated that no need for further intervention was felt (where a referral had been made over child protection concerns), but at other times the prioritisation of risk of abuse meant many other needs were left unmet, including in the aftermath of domestic violence once the mother had separated from the violent partner.

Occasionally a parent felt help offered was too much or the wrong kind. This included more counselling for a child who had been sexually abused (involving in one case starting again with a new service after one had closed) when the mother thought the child wanted to move on and was being overanalysed or was distressed by going over their experience, counselling for a parent who didn't want it and a foster placement for a father whose partner was too ill to look after their children. In the latter case, gendered assumptions may well have influenced the offer – he wanted to look after his children himself and, when he refused fostering, he was left to care for his children with very little support. Interventions to protect children were often seen as too much or the wrong kind of course, but that is in the nature of such interventions. On one occasion, however, when two children had been removed and kept overnight in hospital after a bruise was observed on the boy's leg at school, the father felt his daughter's schoolwork was still affected a year later by the anxiety this had caused her. She was also clearly very guarded in her interview with the researcher, making no mention of any problems at home.

Unlike schools and health services, social services deal predominantly with people living in poverty, to the extent that poverty is so familiar it may easily be taken for granted and forgotten (see Chapter 7 for discussion). Financial pressures on families are now addressed as a part of a full assessment, however, and social workers interviewed described a number of ways they addressed poverty-related issues, including help with benefits, grants and debts, work on budgets and lifestyle issues (such as smoking), and trying to broaden the horizons of young people with a limited sense of their options. They were extremely conscious, however, of the limited extent to which they could address such issues, owing to the lifelong accumulation of disadvantage in many parents' lives and the constraints within which they worked, primarily resource constraints (insufficient funding to meet identified needs), staffing issues (unfilled posts being common) and lack of political commitment (both nationally and, in the affluent areas, where poverty was a little recognised issue, locally). Comments included:

> [T]*he Government's got it all wrong … we should not be penny pinching like we are doing … the impact that we can have on families who are in, in dire financial straits … is quite limited and … sort of spotty, you know, a dot here and a dot there when they hit crisis.*
> (Social worker in affluent area)

> *… lovely legislation, with staff. You can talk all about it, but we currently have six vacancies in our team so there's three people doing the work of nine. Can't do the work if there's not enough people … So you can't do what you can't do. Physically can't work more than ten hours in a day every day of the week. All the legislation in the world would be fantastic, changing the teams and processes, got all these new services. But if you can't staff them they're not going to work.*
> (Social workers in deprived area)

The stresses of social workers' jobs were intensified by a heavy reliance on agency or overseas staff (both of which groups may need support themselves and/or be unable to give much peer support because of lack of familiarity with local policy and procedure and/or lack of experience). The occupational culture was described as one in which it was difficult to say when a worker felt overwhelmed or out of their depth, and the management culture in terms of what Cooper and Lousada (2005) refer to as 'structures of illusion', in which targets are met but needs clearly are not. This gap between appearance and reality caused cynicism about claims of quality, and further frustration at the way work could be distorted (with decisions made to do what can be done within the time limit for which there is a target, rather than to do what is judged best for the situation). Creative work can clearly still occur despite this context, but the frustrations must also sometimes leak into relationships with families.

Different views were expressed about the discouragement of dependency embedded in current policy and practice, one social worker accepting it as appropriate but others seeing it as unhelpful, undermining social workers' ability to meet needs – as one social worker put it: '*we're not dealing with a child that's 14, we're dealing with a parent that could be 35, that this started for that parent 35 years ago, and it's like ... so how are you going to correct that in a short space of time?*' Dependency does seem to be promoted unnecessarily, however, by the difficulties parents have in relation to other services – with parents who cannot afford to make multiple phone calls to benefits, education or housing agencies asking social workers to do it for them. This was a source of frustration – one social worker described parents as wanting to 'offload their responsibilities' – which could easily be remedied, with freephone numbers, for example.

VOLUNTARY ORGANISATIONS AND SELF-HELP GROUPS

Aside from help with benefits, grants and other financial matters (discussed in Chapter 3), participants had accessed a range of forms of help from voluntary organisations, including family support, parenting education courses, childcare, counselling, self-help groups, opportunities to buy cheap clothes and toys, legal advice and refuge when leaving a violent partner. Parenting courses were found helpful for tips and strategies, reassurance and enhancing self-esteem, meeting other parents and increasing authoritativeness, but some had found them ineffective, out of date or not enough. Such classes or courses need to make space for the concerns of parents on them to be addressed and to keep being revised in response to parent input. Experiences of self-help groups were not always positive, but most had valued opportunities for mutual support and sharing of experiences with other parents (in practice mothers), a welcoming atmosphere, an ethos of equality and informality, and opportunities to move on from being a receiver to a giver of help.

Some counselling services either did or seemed to exclude some parents or children, either explicitly by criteria of eligibility or implicitly by the name of the organisation, which did not fit with the person's perceptions of their own or their children's needs. One woman had been recommended to go to the NSPCC when looking for counselling for her son, but felt that his needs were as much related to bereavement, separation and loss as to abuse, so did not take this up. Counsellors within such specialist organisations may be well equipped to address broader concerns than their names indicate, but publicity needs to indicate this if so.

Through many different kinds of voluntary organisation, the most valued service, however, was genuine care for the parent themselves – someone who asked them how they were, who they could talk to, who listened, offered time, reassurance and basic kindness, information and help to access other resources where relevant, and some treats. Except by one parent who was still on their waiting list, the Family Welfare Association was mentioned in universally positive terms. This is probably attributable both specifically to its home visiting service and more broadly to its commitment to an attachment perspective, recognising the need of isolated parents for a service to act as 'secure base'. Very small things could mean a great deal to parents if they were felt to be from someone who 'really cared' – such as a worker from Women's Aid who came round with flowers after a woman had moved into her new home.

THE CRIMINAL JUSTICE SYSTEM

Many (40) participants had had some involvement with the criminal justice system (CJS), for a range of different reasons. When a child had been sexually abused by others (five cases), the police had generally been found supportive to both parent and child, but the later failure to prosecute (in two cases) or convict (in the one case where the perpetrator, an older boy, had been charged) left anger and a sense of the child who was abused having been disbelieved (in one case they did not catch the perpetrator but the family found them very supportive). In the fifth case, where the outcome was not yet known, the family had heard nothing from the police since the investigation four months previously. For those parents (two) who had reported their own experiences of abuse in childhood, there had been a similar sense of betrayal at no action being taken. While evidential requirements still make it difficult to prosecute these kinds of cases successfully, more explanation for parents and children of why such cases are dropped could and should be given.[3]

Women who had reported domestic violence had had mixed experiences. Two cases had resulted in effective action, a conviction in one, a restraining order in the other. Two had not, in one case apparently because of police reluctance to get involved in a domestic situation, the other because the perpetrator was a serving policeman himself and his colleagues had picked him up and dropped him off at his mother's house rather than put him in the cells overnight.

Other reasons for CJS involvement included suspicion of child maltreatment, drugs or other criminal activity by parents (with the full range of outcomes, from no evidence being found and the case being dropped, to conviction and custody) and children getting into trouble. In two cases parents whose children had got into trouble had found unexpectedly good support for themselves in the process, one from a community police officer, the other from a probation officer (in conjunction with a team also involving Connexions and other youth services). In both cases they had found someone they could really talk to about their children, who had offered them support and advice as well as intervening directly with the children.

INTER-AGENCY AND MULTI-AGENCY WORKING

The increased emphasis on multi-agency working is more visible to parents, via such initiatives as Sure Start and Youth Offending Teams, than the longer tradition of inter-agency working (working together to communicate concerns about children and coordinate a response across agencies), though parents occasionally expressed surprise and frustration at the lack of communication, or were angry at information being passed on without informing them or checking out its validity (when a referral was made). This section is therefore based mainly on what professionals in the focus groups said.

In both the affluent and deprived areas there were thought to be pockets of good communication, often linked to particular individuals knowing each other or working on joint projects. Certain schools, health visitors and some GPs were seen as open and committed to working together and joining up services more. Examples of creative practice that were cited included packages of care and support for particular families, health visitors in the affluent area working within schools and SSDs, and a school head seconded with a remit to promote better communication between local services. There was also, however, an overall sense that communication and cooperation between agencies was pretty poor in both areas, with much room for improvement still and a number of constraints.

First, there were clearly still many misunderstandings about other agencies' roles, responsibilities, current capacities or practices, as well as some differences of perception about appropriate action. Social workers, for example, felt workers in other agencies misled parents sometimes about what they would be able to help with, or expected them to take action they could not do (remove a child from home when the criteria were not met, for example). Health visitors also felt they were often perceived as working to a more medical model than they actually did and that, possibly as a result of misunderstanding of their role and possibly because new roles were developing that overlapped with it (e.g. family support workers), they were being left out of many multi-agency forums. The rapid pace of change and information gaps contribute to frustration. Health visitors in London talked of so much going on that most of the time they just didn't know what other agencies were doing. Schools in the affluent area talked of a special educational needs coordinator (SENCo) taking three years to develop a contact list, so that they would know who to contact with a referral, by which time of course both individuals and departments had changed. Several professionals talked of not knowing which other agencies were involved with families they worked with until they found out accidentally.

Second, resource and time constraints clearly interfere with communication both within and between agencies in a range of ways. Social workers talked of different departments withholding information about their responsibilities (e.g. adult services could pay for childcare for a parent having mental health treatment) to protect themselves from costs. Agencies sometimes pass the buck, pushing families backwards and forwards between them, no doubt partly because of underfunding. Referrals are sometimes made to SSDs knowing that nothing will be done, except a note on record, and sometimes require much chasing to find out what is being done (by schools, for example). While social workers didn't always take the time to report back to a school on a referral, one school head had not allowed teachers to attend a core group at SS, presumably for resource reasons.

Third, the emotional impact of the work affects how agencies work together. The families experienced as hardest to work with are those full of anger, conflict and chaos, and where negative patterns of communication, including resistance to any authority figures, are deeply entrenched. These families can easily overwhelm workers and it was thought that they were more likely to be passed on between agencies, undermining the likelihood of effective help being given.

CURRENT DEVELOPMENTS

Recent and current developments that involve agencies working more closely together, including Sure Start, extended schools, children's trusts and common assessment, were mostly seen as positive, at least in principle and potentially in practice. An increased emphasis on prevention in particular was welcomed. Concerns raised, however, included the pace of change, the cosmetic nature of some changes, lack of consultation over priorities or process, the effects of resource constraints and potential loss of expertise in the blurring of roles. Policy documents proliferate at a rapid rate, many much the same as the last one – one health visitor who had recently been studying for a postgraduate degree found it difficult to keep track of it even with that extra time.

The changes involved are long term and it was emphasised that it was a slow process to make the kind of changes envisaged: *'there's a lot to break down for it to work'*, as one social worker said. The targets set for changes to be in place often did not allow sufficient consultation to get them right, but were gone ahead with anyway to comply with government directives. Some changes involved new names for old services or different ways of presenting services, which would not resolve existing problems. Fears were expressed that inter-agency working might get worse, with more need identified and not enough resources to meet it, so that services would be spread even more thinly than they already are, and also that common assessment might mean assessments would be done by people without sufficient expertise and experience to inform their judgements on thresholds for intervention.

The services developing, including Sure Start and extended schools, are clearly increasing resources for many families. In relation to Sure Start, professionals expressed concerns about services that were not always what parents in poverty wanted or needed (e.g. Sure Start offering 'stay and play sessions' when what was needed was rehousing and a home help, or respite at home for families with a number of children of different ages and too much to do already). Some services (e.g. baby massage classes) were also flooded with local middle-class families, which made them intimidating for the isolated families most in need of them who lacked the confidence to come into such an environment. While most parents we interviewed had had positive experiences of Sure Start, if any, and enjoyed the activities on offer, one also had found it unfriendly and unsupportive, and felt staff should take more time to support and befriend women, especially those from different ethnic backgrounds, to help them to integrate into the centre.

The range of services now attached to some schools for parents, including home-school workers, drop-in centres for parents (including those with pre-school children), parenting groups and coffee mornings, wrap-around care, new nurture groups run by speech therapists for children with speech problems and new units for excluded children, were also welcomed. Schools (like GP practices) are places that most parents of children of primary-school age go to, even if they are too depressed or constrained in one way or another to go elsewhere. Schools welcomed the legitimacy a broader role gave them to address problems they had long been aware of (by referring parents on for help) and the opportunity to overcome negative associations that parents might have with schools, though they were aware that such associations, and fears about confidentiality in a school environment, might inhibit take-up. Not all schools wanted to offer extra services, however, and one school head emphasised that *'communication and coordination needs to be really, really thought through'*, if too much is not to fall on headteachers.

There was also a learning curve in how to offer services that were acceptable and accessible, and would be used by parents who needed them. A literacy class located in a school had failed in the affluent areas, requiring parents effectively to go back to school, in a highly visible way – a similar programme had fared better in a community centre context, among other activities. Courses on improving children's behaviour had been welcomed in schools in the deprived areas, but had a high drop-out rate, as parents with conflicting commitments or mental health problems would miss a session or two and then find it difficult to return.

Social workers saw the extra services as a welcome gap-filler, potentially alleviating some of the demands on them for support for parents. Health visitors welcomed the opportunity to see parents in a more social and less medical environment, though still a middle-class one, but feared that the form developments were taking, especially wrap-around care, was too closely linked to the government's agenda of getting parents into work, devaluing and undermining time for parenting. Parents we interviewed had relatively little experience of such developments but were positive about co-located services where they knew of them, especially if the new location brought a service closer to them than it had previously been. It is clear from the comments of both professionals and parents that a range of access points are needed for services, since some parents are more likely to seek help via schools, others via their GPs.

The need to develop services appropriate for culturally diverse communities was an issue in both the affluent and deprived areas. Different minority communities were involved – in our study, they were largely Kosovan refugees and East European migrants in the affluent areas, and a much wider range with a large Bangladeshi community in the deprived areas. Professionals in the deprived areas had considerably more experience of thinking about culturally specific needs, constraints and patterns, but cultural competence is an issue in all contexts and there is a growing literature to inform policy and practice (see, for example, Fontes, 2005; Marjolin, 2005; Connolly *et al.*, 2006).

A number of issues in relation to the Bangladeshi community were highlighted by professionals. A particular generation of women were thought to be especially vulnerable to isolation, especially if living with a violent partner and his parents, without access to independent income or their own passport, and with much family and community pressure not to leave or seek help from agencies. Where women in this position did seek help they sometimes did so for complaints of physical pain, rather than for stress, violence or depression, either lacking a language for, or being inhibited by, the stigma associated with other problems. Lack of confidence in engaging outside the home, combined with the demands of children and domestic work and other pressures, meant women in this position in particular needed services to go to them. An alternative was for them to access services in the places they went to anyway (GPs or schools), at convenient times. First thing in the morning was thought to be preferable, before the daily task of cooking the evening meal from scratch, a cultural tradition that saved money but at the expense of time, had begun. Children in such households had often spent their pre-school years largely within the home and starting school could be particularly daunting for them.

Highlighting such differences carries the danger of setting up new stereotypes and clearly there is much diversity and change within the Bangladeshi or any other BME community, and much overlap between communities. Some families we interviewed had valued very highly specialist support workers from their own community who were familiar with their cultural context, although others preferred to talk to workers outside their own communities for fear of gossip and for confidentiality reasons. Perhaps the most important observation from professionals, however, was the need for them to take time to check out with families what they were able to do, what fitted with their own cultural norms or not, in order to avoid unrealistic expectations of family members based on inaccurate assumptions.

NOTES

1. Although, in many areas, these services have now been redesignated children's services, we use the term parents used, which reflects the period they were discussing.

2. Ghate and Hazel (2002) report having found no evidence that misunderstanding of roles was the explanation. Parents of older children may be more likely to have forgotten, however.

3. The Victim's Charter and the Code of Practice for Victims of Crime set out the current standards that victims of crime should expect. The police should check with victims if they want information about the progress of a case, and provide it if they do. The Crown Prosecution Service now has an obligation to meet with victims of serious offences (including child abuse and sexual offences) to explain their decisions if they do not prosecute, or if a charge is dropped or substantially changed (or to provide reasons in writing for not doing so if they decide not to).

Risk and resilience in low-income families – case studies and reflections

KEY POINTS

- There is a known association between poverty and some forms of child maltreatment (neglect and physical abuse), established by other research, although many other factors contribute to risk and the vast majority of parents living in poverty do not maltreat their children.

- By some definitions, poverty is itself a form of child abuse. We argue for maintaining distinctions between different forms of harm. The study supports the argument that child poverty is a form of societal neglect, however.

- The most common perspective on the relationship between poverty and maltreatment focuses on stress, sometimes linked to poor neighbourhoods, with social support as a key factor in resilience. The accounts of incidents of maltreatment given in this study support the relevance of stress, and also suggest other concepts and issues that merit more attention in future research. These are:
  - parents' experiences of violence and abuse, which may have ongoing impacts on their lives, which are much more complex than implied by 'cycle of abuse' arguments, and which are interwoven with poverty in a range of ways
  - parents' experiences of attachment and the ongoing conflicts over care and control associated with insecurity, which may be compounded or made difficult to resolve by poverty
  - defensive investments in identity as a parent reflecting lack of alternatives as a result of poverty, and spoiled identities associated with poverty and other life experiences, both of which may contribute to social isolation
  - the need for recognition and respect, often denied people living in poverty and those who experience other forms of adversity, especially violence and abuse, which may make children's behaviour problems (and sometimes ordinary lack of respect) difficult to bear or manage
  - the impact of resources (along with other factors such as drug use or mental health problems) on the risks taken with children's supervision
  - the impact of the bodily experience of childbearing on women's relationships with children, especially where children are born as a result of rape, with poverty allowing little relief from such difficult relationships
  - the impact of the child as an actor whose expressed wishes (e.g. regarding contact with non-resident fathers) and responses to distress (e.g. by running away, self-harming or being violent to siblings) may impede parents' capacity to protect both that child and others, especially when financial, social and personal resources are overstretched
  - the role of services, where negative experiences may compound family members' isolation and powerlessness – the lack of resources to meet assessed need and the

(Continued)

separation of youth justice from other services for children are particular ongoing concerns.

- There was little evidence that professionals see as neglect what is only poverty. In discussions of neglect in families, poverty often slipped out of sight, however, as professionals focused instead on other risk factors such as drug and alcohol problems, and on individual attitudes, values and priorities. A limited conception of poverty, lack of resources to address it, and lack of attention to the impacts of trauma, addiction and lifelong disadvantage on the choices that people experience themselves as having may contribute to overemphasising agency at the expense of structural inequality.

This chapter returns to the initial aim of the project – to increase understanding of the known association between poverty and some forms of child maltreatment (neglect and to a lesser extent physical abuse). This association has been found both at the household (Cawson *et al.*, 2000; Sidebotham *et al.*, 2002; Sidebotham and Heron, 2006) and at the neighbourhood levels (Drake and Pandey, 1996; Gillham *et al.*, 1998), although existing research is all limited in one way or another by the indicators used, both of poverty or neighbourhood deprivation and of child maltreatment. The best source of data in the UK is now the NSPCC's prevalence study, for which a random sample of 2,689 18–24 year olds were interviewed about their childhood experiences (Cawson *et al.*, 2000). Young people in semi-skilled or unskilled employment were three times more likely to have suffered serious physical abuse and ten times more likely to have experienced serious absence of care in childhood than respondents in professional jobs. They were also twice as likely to have experienced serious absence of care than respondents in higher education. It is possible of course that childhood abuse had depressed educational attainment and hence employment opportunities later, at least for some. However, respondents were also asked to agree or not with a statement that 'there were always a lot of worries about shortage of money' in their families when they were children. Thirty-four per cent of all respondents agreed with this, but 65 per cent of those assessed as experiencing serious physical abuse and serious absence of care agreed with it. Seventy-one per cent of those assessed as experiencing emotional maltreatment also agreed with it, although no social class trends were identified for emotional maltreatment using other indicators. A preliminary analysis of the Millenium Cohort Survey when the children were aged three has also found that shouting at children, though not smacking, is associated with poverty (Kiernan, 2006).

It is worth restating that the vast majority of parents living in poverty do not abuse or neglect their children, and there is an extensive literature identifying other factors that contribute to risk. The ecological model proposed by Bronfenbrenner (1979) is now widely accepted and Sidebotham and Heron (2006) have recently summarised the evidence on risk factors for maltreatment, which include young parents, lone parents, the presence of a step-parent (especially for child sexual abuse), large families, domestic violence, parents with low educational achievements, parents with adverse childhood experiences (including abuse) themselves, parents with a psychiatric history (including a history of alcohol or drug abuse), paternal unemployment, poor social networks, unwanted children and children whose parents report few positive attributes to them, babies of low birth weight and children with health, behaviour or developmental problems, and disabled children. There are more mixed findings on maternal employment and/or unemployment, probably reflecting the more complex and variable relationship that women have to paid work. Gelles (1987) found that, while mothers' employment itself was not associated with increased violence to children, lack of choice over whether to work and a sense of having excess responsibility for domestic activities alongside paid work was. More recent research tends towards finding maternal unemployment rather than employment associated with risk, probably reflecting the increased labour-force participation among women with children and the consequent changing meaning of unemployment (Sidebotham *et al.*, 2002).

Research on resilience or protective factors is less well developed but also growing (see, for example, Gilligan, 2004, 2006; Daniel, 2006). The main recurring theme here is that social support from a partner, relatives or friends is protective, although perceptions of support being available are as important as the extent of networks and the support actually received (Sidebotham, *et al.*, 2002; Sidebotham and Heron, 2006)

It is not our aim to add to the literature identifying risk or resilience factors, for two reasons. First, there are many studies better designed to do that. While much research in this field relies on partial and not wholly reliable information – e.g. Child Protection Registration, the limitations of which as a measure of maltreatment are well-known – our data on maltreatment comprises the accounts given by our research participants. These were often limited by memory and/or defensiveness, and occasionally included incidents the definition of which as abuse or not was contested (either between the parent and SSD or the parent and someone else, such as another child's parent). Second, a preoccupation with risk factors abstracted from contexts and the meaning attributed to them itself has risks of losing sight of the person at the heart of them. The traditional social work role of mediating between clients' subjective experience and the objective categories around which law and policy are constructed is seriously undermined if this occurs, as is the more recent goal of a holistic approach to families. The emotional complexity of the work of intervening in families may also be lost sight of in this rationalist approach, which reduces the complexities of family life to a matter of technical measurement.

The strength of a qualitative approach is to maintain a focus on context and meaning through detailed accounts, and to ground the exploration of new concepts and the identification of new issues that may be relevant in the perspectives of participants. Life history interviewing also allows a holistic approach to the issues addressed and their development over time. After a brief summary of the incidents of maltreatment within our sample, we therefore start this chapter with four case studies of families in which both risk and resilience were present. In each, one or more incident(s) clearly identifiable as child maltreatment have occurred, but there is much more to the families' stories than that. In the second half of the chapter we use our data to reflect on current theorising of the association between poverty and maltreatment, and identify issues that merit more attention in future research and practice.

CHILD MALTREATMENT IN OUR SAMPLE

The National Commission of Inquiry into the Prevention of Child Abuse gave the following definition:

> *Child abuse consists of anything which individuals, institutions or processes do or fail to do which directly or indirectly harms children or damages their prospects of safe and healthy development into adulthood.*
> (National Commission of Inquiry into the Prevention of Child Abuse, 1996, p. 2)

By such a definition, poverty is itself a form of abuse and all the children in our sample were affected. Such a broad definition has limitations, however. Harm attributable to individuals with whom a child has direct contact (as in more common definitions) is likely to have a different meaning and impact from harm attributable to central or local government action or inaction, and to require different forms of intervention. The evidence from our study and many others on the range of harms that children living in poverty experience gives strong support to the argument that poverty should at least be seen as a form of societal neglect (Dubowitz, 2006). In this section, however, we use child maltreatment to refer to physical abuse, sexual abuse, emotional abuse and neglect, the forms of abuse defined in government guidance (HM Government, 2006b).

Of the 70 households in our study, there was some incident of maltreatment, including exposure to domestic violence, sexual abuse (intra and extrafamilial) and sibling abuse in 44, although only 12 households had ever had a child on the Child Protection Register. In some of the households there had been several forms of maltreatment – in particular domestic violence was often the context of neglect, physical abuse (either where children were caught in the crossfire or where abuse of the child was an extension of violence to the mother) and sometimes sexual abuse. Exposure to domestic violence is now recognised as a form of emotional abuse, and the terrifying impact of witnessing it, ongoing fear of its recurrence and the responsibility children sometimes felt for protecting their mothers all illustrate this. One woman's violent partner had also told his children he was beating their mother (in front of them) to punish her for her failings in relation to them, making them complicit in their mother's abuse.

Domestic violence was also often the context of the development of children's violence to their mothers, their siblings or themselves. Where children's self-harm, risky behaviour or aggression was not causing direct harm to others in the family, we did not include it in the maltreatment figures, though the boundary is not entirely clear, e.g. one child was not causing harm only because he was too small and slight to do so. There was also considerable emotional neglect from separated fathers, which we did not include in these figures. In some cases links to stress and poverty were obvious, in others much less so, although in the cases in this sample they were inevitably part of the background.

CASE STUDIES

CASE STUDY **1**   Susanne Millard grew up in a relatively affluent middle-class family. She had mixed experiences of care in her childhood and a particularly difficult relationship with her mother. Susanne did a degree in engineering and then managed pubs for a while. She married, had two children and was the main breadwinner for her family, working long hours while her husband stayed at home with the children. She dropped into poverty after going bankrupt, taking a lower-paid job, having a third child and being made redundant again while pregnant so that she had no maternity cover. After the birth she suffered from post-natal depression and was finding it so difficult to cope that she sought support from social services. Her husband, who had rarely worked, was spending a lot of their income on drinking and fishing equipment, and his physical and emotional violence against her and their children was increasing. He resisted all the efforts of social services to support them. One day he disappeared, leaving Susanne suddenly a lone mother of three young children, entirely dependent on benefits and with family debts to pay off.

Susanne now lives on a quiet, new housing association estate with her daughters (11 and five years) and son (nine years). She still suffers from depression and her self-esteem was badly affected by falling into poverty and by the emotional abuse she suffered from her mother and her husband, both of which have continued (her husband is now back in contact). She feels a strong sense of having failed, particularly in the context of her family, as her parents and siblings are mostly professionals with middle-class incomes and lifestyles. She finds it hard to afford to socialise with her old friends and humiliated when they try to support her by refusing to allow her to buy a round. Her self-respect is clearly very much rooted in paying her own way.

She works 16 hours per week doing the books for, and behind the bar of, a local social club. She works for her own self-respect, because it gives her some respite from the stress of her home life and contact with work-based friends, and in the hope that it will improve her future earning prospects. She is actually slightly worse off financially and struggles to manage her time and financial commitments, feeling that she never stops yet is never on top of anything.

She was recently reported twice by her mother to social services for separate incidents. The first incident happened when her oldest daughter sneaked into her room, stole some chocolate she had hidden there, ate it, then lied to her about it. When she found the wrappers in her daughter's bedroom, she 'lost it' and hit her and, feeling terrible, then called her sister and asked her to come and get her daughter while they cooled off. This incident seemed to have much to do with the significance of the chocolate as something of her own, a gift given by a friend and prized in the context of the scarcity and deprivation of everyday life. It also seemed to be partly a response to feeling disrespected by her daughter when her self-respect was very fragile. The second incident occurred when her usual babysitter let her down when she was due to work an evening shift. She didn't want to risk losing the job or the income and had no one else she could ask, so left the oldest child in charge with a phone, telling her to call her or go to a neighbour if there was any problem. In both cases, her mother found out and reported her to social services without discussing it with Susanne or offering any help. Having discussed the full circumstances of each case with her social worker, Susanne felt quite supported by them but also angry and distressed by her mother's actions. The incidents had served to emphasise the lack of support she receives from her mother.

Susanne has been attending regular counselling for over two years and has recently decided to have no more contact with her mother in recognition that the relationship was more a source of stress than support. She has also decided to limit contact with her ex-husband and try to minimise the impact of his emotionally abusive verbal attacks. This had been a very important decision for her and she was feeling for the first time in years that her life might become more manageable.

CASE STUDY 2   David Shipley grew up in an affluent but unhappy home. His father was physically violent and both parents were controlling and emotionally abusive, favouring his older sister, the '*golden girl*'. At 16 he left home: '*I had to get away from my parents, if I'm honest I think either my father would have killed me or even worse I would have probably killed him*'.

After an early marriage, which failed quickly, David married a second time and had two children. He had his own transport business and worked long hours but had a very comfortable income. He was diagnosed with bi-polar disorder, however, and the medication prevented him from driving, although he continued to manage the business. His marriage broke down and his wife left him with the children, then five and three years old. He gave up work to care for his children full time and found it extremely difficult to cope with the sharp drop in income and change in lifestyle. He lost his business and built up so many debts that he eventually had to declare himself bankrupt.

David felt very isolated, struggling with the challenges of parenting on a low income and suffering bouts of severe depression. He found that structures helped him to cope and feel in control, and he imposed strict routines on himself and the children, and had detailed systems for managing his income and expenditure. He experienced the stigma of being on a low income very keenly and felt he was viewed by society as '*scum of the earth*', condemned for being unemployed and dependent on benefits without regard for the circumstances that had contributed to his situation. He had repeatedly approached services for help but had been reassured that he was coping fine. He described having felt like '*a bloke drowning at sea*', frantically waving for help with people waving back cheerfully and passing by, not able to see that he was about to go under.

David's son, now eight years old, was regularly wetting his bed and David had become concerned about it. The doctor had advised a regime of regular drinks during the day to stretch the bladder and nothing to drink after 6.00 p.m. David was determined that his son should stick to the regime and felt that keeping him to it was the only way he could help him with this problem. When his son didn't stick to the drinking regime, David attributed it partly to laziness and partly to not wanting to stand out at school. He confronted his son but his son denied missing drinks, and David became so angry that he hit his son on the leg. He felt that this had got the message through to him that keeping to the regime was important. A teacher then noticed the mark on his son's leg and reported it to social services. The first that David and his family knew of this was when a social worker arrived with police that evening, arrested David and took his two children into temporary care. David said he had understood from the police that, if he pleaded guilty to assaulting his son and agreed to receive support from social services, his children would be returned home and the family reunited the next day, but, if he did not, he would not be allowed to see his children for six months until the case could be brought to trial. David pleaded guilty to the charges, although he still did not believe that he had done anything wrong.

Although the intervention by social services was traumatic for David and his children, it had some positive outcomes. For the first time David felt he was receiving the help he had been seeking almost since becoming a lone parent. The most important element was that he was found to be eligible for disability living allowance, which gave him a small increase in income. He used this to have private treatment for his mental health problems. His new psychiatrist changed his diagnosis to a personality disorder related to childhood abuse experiences, which much more closely matches David's own perceptions of his condition, and took him off unnecessary medication. David still has to contend with harassment from his parents (who own the house where he lives) and is not sure that he will ever be able to work again, which he finds demoralising. However, he feels hopeful because some of his personal issues are finally being addressed, he is happy in a new relationship and has high aspirations for his children.

CASE STUDY **3**   Bhashkar and Rani Gopal live in a deprived area of London with their four children. They were both born in Bangladesh and came to the UK separately in their early 20s. Bhashkar's parents came to the UK when he was seven, leaving him behind in Bangladesh with relatives. He felt abandoned and insecure, and there was no one he was close to as he grew up. At 22, he joined his parents and younger siblings born in the UK, but found them unwelcoming and distant. He no longer has contact with his family and is haunted by a sense of loss from this childhood experience. Rani had a loving relationship with her mother and siblings, although her father was strict and put pressure on them to do well academically, and was sometimes an angry and intimidating figure. Rani's parents and siblings still live in Bangladesh and she has little contact with them. She has an aunt living in this country who she talks to regularly and who provides practical help and childcare.

Eight years ago Rani began to find it hard to sleep and lost her appetite. She went to her GP and was diagnosed with depression and given sleeping tablets. These did not help and over the next two years her condition got progressively worse, she was hearing voices, becoming aggressive towards her children and losing her self-awareness. Despite regular visits to her GP it seems her condition was not taken seriously and she received little help. Finally she had what was probably a psychotic episode, which she now has little memory of, in which she threatened to burn her children and to kill herself with a knife in front of them. She was admitted to a psychiatric ward and stayed for almost two months. Social services became involved and offered to place the children in temporary foster care but Bhashkar was adamant that the children should stay with him, and gave up his job to stay home and care for his children and wife.

Bhashkar had earned a reasonable income from his work at a factory but, after this crisis, the family became dependent on benefits. Bhashkar found it very difficult at first, having no idea what benefits they might be entitled to or where to go to get advice. He found their social worker of limited help and they missed out on some benefits they were entitled to at first. They have had better support from their Family Welfare Association Bangladeshi support worker who visits regularly and helps them access services and grants. They still have to go and see the social worker at his office every three to four months.

Rani and Bhashkar both liked the first psychiatrist who cared for Rani, visiting her together, finding her very understanding and appreciating the presence of the interpreter provided. However, Rani has since been reassigned to a new psychiatrist who they are less happy with. He only sees her once every three months and appointments are sometimes given at inconvenient times, which she cannot attend. Rani has been referred to support groups but is unwilling to attend because of the particularly high stigma associated with mental health problems within the Bangladeshi community.

The children were very frightened by their mother's illness and would stay in their bedrooms, avoiding her for a while. They still tend to keep out of her way. Bhashkar believes (or hopes) the children have not been too badly affected by their mother's illness and feels things are better for them now she is stable, but they have never spoken openly about the illness or the times when she threatened to harm them or herself. His 11-year-old son worries about his mother and the stress that he sees his parents are under. He talked of feeling he may be partly responsible and of needing to behave well so as not to add to their stress. None of the children has received any counselling or support aimed at addressing their experiences of their mother's illness.

Bhashkar and Rani are each other's main source of support and both take pride in their children. Bhaskar feels it was his need to protect and care for his children that gave him the strength to cope with the crisis of his wife's breakdown and the subsequent change in lifestyle. He also feels supported by his Islamic faith and its teachings on how to be a good parent through loving and being there for his children. He has recently joined a carers' support group and has been doing voluntary work with older people at his local community centre. He has now started training with them, which he enjoys and this has boosted his self-esteem.

CASE STUDY **4**   Anna James is a lone mother of three children, twins (girl and boy) aged 11 and an older son of 21 who no longer lives with them. Anna had a very insecure childhood. Her father was emotionally abusive and her mother left him when she was two years old, moving them right across the country. She has not seen him since. Her mother did her best, but she was not very affectionate. Anna was often afraid as a child, partly because they lived in temporary accommodation with violent neighbours for a long time, and she grew into an unconfident teenager.

At 17 Anna became involved with her first partner and had her oldest son. Her partner was physically and emotionally abusive to her and she left him when their son was two and moved back in with her mother. Her second partner, with whom she had the twins, was also violent. She sent her oldest son to live with her mother because she was concerned about his safety but her son felt rejected and jealous of the twins. She began to feel her partner was mentally ill and tried to get help from his GP, but her partner countered with an accusation about her to social services and she found they didn't take her concerns seriously. She tried to leave him but without success and continued to suffer his violence. Finally her partner punched her in the nose in public and, as a result of this incident, which was witnessed, he was sectioned and she was able to get an injunction and some help to move to a new area. The twins were one at the time. Her partner was eventually diagnosed with paranoid schizophrenia.

Anna's oldest son, then 11, returned to live with them. She has always found him difficult but, from the time he started living with his grandmother, his behaviour with his mother grew progressively worse. When he returned home he was aggressive, violent and controlling towards her, and very jealous of his younger siblings, whom he bullied. He smashed up the home and was frequently excluded from school. She felt victimised again and unable to manage her son's behaviour or adequately protect her twins. She sought help from social services but felt they did not recognise the severity of the situation and did little to help. On one occasion she threatened in frustration to kill him, hoping to elicit a greater response, and social services did find someone for her to talk to, but nothing further came of it. Anna feels she was left very much alone with this problem, which was only relieved when her son moved out. He still visits and, although his sometimes controlling behaviour towards her continues, she feels their relationship is improving.

Anna's youngest son, now 11, is also showing aggressive and violent behavioural problems. Anna is afraid both that he is following behaviour patterns learned from his older brother and that he may have inherited mental health problems from his father. This son calls her '*fat and ugly*', which she finds very upsetting, and tries to control (limit) her eating. He is also aggressive towards his twin sister, frequently fighting with her and hitting her hard enough to bruise. His sister is upset by this and also feels that she and her mother are both powerless to stop her brother hurting them. She no longer tells her mother when he upsets her as '*nothing can be done*' but instead goes to her bedroom and cries alone.

Anna feels she has quite a good support network of friends and a close relationship with her own mother and brothers, but her sons' abusive behaviour towards her undermines her self-confidence and she feels like a failure, particularly when she gets angry and shouts at her younger son. Their behaviour and lack of money are the most stressful aspects of her life. She also feels people treat her differently, not because of being poor but because of being a lone parent, not working and with children of mixed race. She feels she manages because there is no other choice and she tries to do what she can to make the children happy and help them be confident. She wants them to do better than she has.

Although her son's behavioural problems remain extreme and very difficult to deal with, Anna has much better support from services this time than with her first son. She was referred by social services to Connexions and a young offenders team, and has a good relationship with a worker from each. She sees at least one every other week and, although her son is resisting talking to them, she finds it a great support for herself and her efforts to manage his behaviour. She and her twins particularly like one worker who is non-judgemental, doesn't make a big deal out of anything but laughs with them and makes them feel on the same level with him. She also feels supported by a worker from a local housing charity who helped her apply for tax credits and increase their income: '*I feel support … like a circle of support. Like never before you know.*'

RETHINKING THE LINK BETWEEN POVERTY AND MALTREATMENT

The main perspectives on the link between poverty and maltreatment identified by Katz (2004); Katz *et al.* (2007, forthcoming) are the following.

1. *Stress*: that the stresses of living on a low income, especially when combined with other issues such as drug abuse or mental health problems (both of which may be linked to poverty), may lead parents to react to the demands of looking after children with harsh or inconsistent discipline, or sink into depression, despair and hopelessness, and neglect their needs. The role of social support in resilience is explained by its ability to buffer the impacts of stressful life events.

2. *Culture*: culture of poverty arguments link poverty, neglect and child abuse through the assumption that the parents concerned have different values from the mainstream, in which physical discipline and lower standards of supervision are acceptable. This is essentially the concept of an underclass, in which criminality and low educational attainment are also sometimes cited, and linked to lone parenthood.

Poor neighbourhoods have been linked to both arguments as the source of additional stresses (e.g. via high crime, poor housing and amenities, etc.) or the location of subcultural norms. The most common argument now is the stress (and resilience) one, often combined with poor neighbourhoods. Parents in poor neighbourhoods have been found to report higher levels of stress (Ghate and Hazel, 2002; Barnes *et al.*, no date) and there is a growing emphasis on community-level interventions, e.g. building social capital and social networks to promote resilience (Jack, 2000, 2004, 2006). The 'culture of poverty' argument is given much less credence now, partly because of its normative assumptions and right-wing associations, and partly because of the lack of evidence to support it. New thinking on the social relations dimensions of poverty suggests other ways of thinking about culture, however, which have begun to be explored (e.g. Tuck, 2000) and we build on these below.

Our data supports the argument that stress, unless buffered by sufficient social support and/or mitigated by other sources of resilience, is likely to be significant in the increased risk of some forms of maltreatment among parents living in poverty. Drawing on a range of other literatures, alongside our data, there are also a number of other (overlapping) issues and concepts that merit more attention. The remainder of this chapter necessarily recaps some of the analysis in earlier chapters.

VIOLENCE AND ABUSE   The increased risk of maltreatment associated with parents' own histories of abuse in childhood and with domestic violence is well established (see, for example, Egeland, 1993; Kaufman and Zigler, 1993; Mullender, 1996; McGuigan and Pratt, 2001). The idea of a 'cycle of abuse' is misleadingly overdeterministic, however, and unhelpful in terms of recognising the processes involved. Current thinking on the role of trauma in the onset of mental health problems (Department of Health, 2002) and the impacts of mental health problems, especially depression (Sheppard, 1994, 2001) and dissociation (Egeland and Susman-Stillman, 1996; Benjamin *et al.*, 1998), on parenting is more useful.

Interactions with poverty occurred in a number of ways in our sample. First, for some women, poverty was a direct consequence of violence, where they had become lone parents after leaving a violent partner. In this context, risks to children sometimes continued from non-resident fathers, as described above. Second, for some parents, men and women, financial and/or emotional abuse was ongoing, from ex-partners and/or from parents. Histories of abuse and such ongoing conflicts could affect people's ability to gain control over their lives, and managing both finances and children with any authority could be a struggle in this context. Third, access to the 'buffer zone' of social and financial support from extended families, which helps many to cope with poverty, was often limited or non-existent for those with histories of childhood maltreatment. The capacity to generate social support or to access practical help elsewhere could also be inhibited by the impacts of abuse on trust and intimacy ('trauma isolates', as Herman (1992) puts it), by the effects of poverty on opportunity and by the stigma attached to both abuse and poverty. Fourth, the impacts of abuse on mental health may be compounded by poverty – the very high levels of depression among women with children living in poverty are well known (Brown and Harris, 1978; Sheppard, 1994, 2001).

ATTACHMENT INSECURITY AND CARE AND CONTROL CONFLICTS   Histories of childhood abuse affect parenting partly by the impact of abuse on attachment, which plays a crucial role in the development of caregiving capacity (Heard and Lake, 1997). Children who lack secure attachment(s) are more vulnerable to abuse and abuse may in turn contribute to insecure attachment. Children who are or become insecure may, unless they have access to supportive relationships that enable them to rework their internal models of experience in relationship, become insecure parents. Insecure parents in turn are more likely to have insecure children, and so on, although none of this is inevitable. The impact of insecure childhood attachment on adults can be observed as 'unresolved care and control conflicts', common among parents who abuse their children (Reder and Duncan, 2001). These will affect how people respond to threats to their own well-being in terms of the dynamics of attachment that continue throughout life (Heard and Lake, 1997). Where care-seeking has been met by effective caregiving in childhood (or later), people will tend either to self-care or to seek care in response to threat in a way that elicits it again if they need it. If it is available, and their needs are assuaged, they will be able to continue caregiving for their children. Where it has not, they are more likely either to continue care-seeking, often in distorted or ineffective ways, or go into self-defence, both of which will undermine their ability to respond effectively to their children's needs for care.

Poverty may compound the impacts of internal conflicts or make it difficult to resolve them, as well as to meet ongoing needs. Care is often unavailable, e.g. where informal support is affected by lack of resources to socialise, and formal support such as counselling costs too much, or comes with the risk of loss of control, from statutory interventions in mental health or child protection. Control over fundamental aspects of life, e.g. housing and income, may be impossible to gain. Since living in poverty involves multiple threats to well-being and high levels of uncertainty, over the availability of resources to meet needs, over safety in high crime neighbourhoods, over poor health, over temporary housing, etc., attachment is also highly relevant to how people manage it (Marris, 1996). This makes sense of findings on social support, which show that 'feeling supported' (Ghate and Hazel, 2002) is the critical factor in buffering stress and 'satisfaction with social support' in enabling authoritative parenting (Ruscio, 2001). For support to be effective it requires a particular kind of interaction, not simply the presence of a social network (McCluskey, 2005). The significance of perceptions of support being available beyond its actual use also reflects the attachment concept of a 'secure base'.

IDENTITIES
Thinking about gender, violence and parenting has addressed issues of social identity, in terms of the greater legitimacy of violence associated with masculinity and the overwhelming sense of responsibility associated with cultural constructions of motherhood. Early motherhood is also a way in which young women in deprived environments, with few other opportunities, find a socially valued role. While the meaning and purpose they find in it may be a source of resilience if they are adequately supported (as McDermott *et al.*, 2004 note), their investment in the identity of mother may also be defensive and idealised, appearing to offer not only a valued role but also a new start after troubled childhoods. In this context, admitting to any 'failure' or need for help can be felt as highly threatening, compounding the isolation that is known to increase the risk of maltreatment. The same may also be true for some young fathers, as fatherhood comes to offer more of an alternative identity to paid work for men. The stigma attached to histories of abuse and mental health problems, for example, compounds the problem, and may be reinforced by professional responses where a 'risk factor' approach to intervention offers no alternative to a negative evaluation of such experiences. One women in our study had spoken to a counsellor of being sexually abused by her grandfather and stepfather as a child, and had apparently been told she would need counselling for the rest of her life – she never went back.

RECOGNITION AND
RESPECT
As well as adequate material resources, recognition and respect are fundamental human needs commonly denied to marginalised and oppressed groups (Fraser, 1997; Lister, 2004). In the field of crime, violent offending can sometimes be an attempt to gain respect by people for whom it has been in short supply, either by intimidation of the victim or by the gaining of status with peers (Batchelor, 2005; Barry, 2006). Our data suggests

that similar issues are also sometimes the context of abuse in the family, where fairly ordinary misbehaviour of children can be experienced as yet another painful experience of disrespect on top of histories of abuse and a sense of being devalued and stigmatised in the wider world, and can trigger violence in response. This was most clearly articulated by parents who had dropped into poverty from a middle-class background through some kind of (or several) misfortune(s). In case study 1, for example, the mother found her self-respect continually undermined by the keenly felt deprivations of living in poverty and in her relationships with her mother and ex-partner. In this context, when her daughter stole some chocolate she had been given as a present from her bedroom, and then lied to her about it, she had hit her. She was clear that this was not about the chocolate itself (she was diabetic and could not eat it) but about her daughter's apparent disrespect for her and for something that belonged to her.

RISKS AND RESOURCES

Some risks have to be taken in parenting in order to balance the protection, supervision and care of children with the need to respect and promote their developing autonomy. The risks taken were sometimes affected by lack of resources (e.g. lack of affordable childcare meaning older children were left to care for younger siblings, or children were left with alternatives who proved unreliable), conflicting responsibilities (between parenting and work, the context in which this sometimes occurred) and/or conflicting relationships (sometimes between the mother's relationships with partner and child, but most problematically between two siblings, where one was a risk to the other). Perceptions of risk were clearly distorted in some cases by drug use or mental health problems – e.g. where parents thought they or their children were coping – and judgements may be better or worse for a variety of reasons. They may clearly be affected by lack of the alternative options that resources can buy.

THE BODY

Much of the literature on gender and parenting focuses on gendered responsibilities and identities. The bodily experience of childbearing may also retain a lasting relevance to women's relationships to their children, however. In four cases in our study, a child had been born as the result of rape, and three of these relationships remained difficult, charged with the memory of their origin. In another case, the relationship was difficult because the mother blamed a first child for the miscarriage of her much-wanted second child, which had happened the day after she carried the first child downstairs. In a fifth, a particularly severe bout of post-natal depression, resulting in violent fantasies and temporary separation from the child for his safety, had taken its toll on the relationship. These were the five cases in which emotional abuse was linked primarily to the meaning of the child – while these situations can happen in any economic context, scarce resources make them more difficult to manage, with little opportunity for relief.

INTERACTION WITH THE CHILD

There has been relatively little exploration so far of what Katz *et al.* (2007, forthcoming) call the 'bidirectionality' of parenting, though Ghate and Hazel (2002) found parents were more stressed when they reported having 'difficult children'. Lack of attention to this issue is a reflection partly of the real power parents have over children and the necessary responsibilities this entails, and partly of socially constructed notions of parental responsibility (an ever-expanding concept, especially in relation to motherhood), and of childhood innocence, which may appear to deny children any agency or influence at all. There were a number of ways in which the child could be an actor in the context in which risks were taken and/or abuse occurred in our study. To acknowledge this is not to attribute responsibility for abuse to the child, but simply to recognise an important part of the context in which abuse may occur, and one potential source of limits to the parent's, usually the mother's, capacity to protect her children.

First, children had their own views and wishes regarding continued contact with separated fathers, including those who had been violent either to their mother or to them in the past. Where they wanted contact and the mother agreed, further abuse sometimes occurred. Second, children who ran away from home were difficult to supervise effectively. Running away may be a response to a range of issues, past and present. One child who got out of the house whenever he could, including escaping through bedroom windows, explained it in terms of feeling bored and restricted at home. His mother thought he was trying to get to his father who had recently left. Her own relationship with him had also always been difficult, having started with a period of severe post-natal depression. Third, children's behaviour problems, often thought to be a response to domestic violence or some early loss or disruption, e.g. a father's death, could create direct risks to other children, and/or indirect risks via their impact on the mother, through causing her distress and undermining her confidence, and through diverting her attention from other children to cope with them. Again these situations can occur in any economic context, but are harder to manage without the resources to gain relief and when energy is depleted by stress and/or mental health problems.

THE ROLE OF SERVICES

Services are rarely included in factors that may increase risk as well as build resilience. The concept of social exclusion draws attention to services, however, in terms of both barriers to access and institutional processes that may systematically marginalise or exclude certain groups. Services are unlikely ever to be able to resolve all problems, some of which are very intractable but, as the last chapter showed, many families had mixed experience of services. Negative experiences could inhibit further help-seeking and/or engagement with services. Many improvements are now going on in children's services, and the concluding chapter returns to these and some of the tensions within current policy. Here it is worth noting two points.

First, the role of resources to meet identified need is crucial. It is not enough to assess risk or need and then leave families waiting for months before they receive a service or are told that they are too low priority to receive one at all. The situation of families who had been investigated for child protection concerns and been offered no service when concerns were unsubstantiated was highlighted in a different context over a decade ago (Department of Health, 1995). While the assessment framework and process is much more comprehensive and broad-based now, the effect on families of being left without help, despite substantial professional intervention, may sometimes be worse, adding to their sense of hopelessness and desperation.

Second, without considerable extra investment, it is unlikely that children's services will be able to move to the more holistic, preventative approach envisaged in policy, given the current climate of public anxiety about child abuse and child deaths, and the statutory responsibilities of agencies for children at risk of significant harm. In that case, parents may continue to be frustrated that '*you have to hit your child to get any help*'. A more holistic approach may also be inhibited by the continued division between youth justice and other services for children and families in this country, which is easily forgotten in the current drive towards integration of social services, education and health. In most other European countries and Scotland, children and young people's offending is dealt with alongside other family problems.

IMPLICATIONS – REINSTATING POVERTY AWARENESS IN ANTI-OPPRESSIVE PRACTICE

Parents sometimes think that professionals see as neglect what is really just poverty. Professionals we interviewed were confident (and convincingly so) that they did not, although they were concerned that middle-class neglect was less likely to be recognised than 'the kind of neglect' associated with poverty. Where resources are scarce and thresholds for intervention high, poverty alone is unlikely to be enough to trigger concern. However, in making the distinction between poor families in which children are adequately cared for and those in which they are not, poverty itself often slipped out of sight in relation to the latter as they focused instead on 'the other things' that made the difference, often parents' priorities, values and attitudes as well as known risk factors (such as drug problems). This partly reflects a conception of poverty that focuses only on income. The conclusion that more money *alone* would not resolve all problems (which is probably true, though in most cases it would certainly be of benefit) helps to divert attention from the structural context of inequality and long-term lack of opportunity, which has impacts beyond the immediate availability of money. Attention is focused instead on the individual and their attitudes, with an emphasis on agency which can obscure the impact of trauma, addiction and/or multiple disadvantage on the choices people experience themselves as having. While many professionals clearly recognised the accumulation of disadvantage over years, or even generations, and its impact, the lack of resources they have to address it may also lead to frustration, which tips the balance into overemphasising individual agency. The sense that some parents express that they are being judged for being poor may be the result, partly of these processes and of the broader 'othering' of 'the poor' discussed in Chapter 1, as well as (sometimes) parents' reluctance to acknowledge their other problems.

For well over a decade, social workers have been required to work anti-oppressively, i.e. to recognise the structural constraints affecting their clients' lives. Less attention is often paid in training now to poverty and class than to the more recently recognised issues of gender, 'race', ethnicity and disability, however. One implication of our research is the need for social work education, and training for other professional groups (via the new National Academy for Parenting Professionals, for example), to pay more attention to the many ways in which poverty (in its broadest concept) affects parents' lives.

8 *Concluding comments and recommendations*

Happy families are all alike; every unhappy family is unhappy in its own way.
(Leo Tolstoy, *Anna Karenina*)

Tolstoy's well-known line captures a key message from our participants – that each family, and each individual within it, has their own unique story. While this is in a sense obvious, it is easily lost sight of in the language of current policy in which risk factors are abstracted from context and meaning, and high-risk families are assumed to be identifiable with very brief checklists to enable interventions to be targeted on them (HM Government, 2006a). The language changes – from 'multi-problem families', to 'high harm and high cost',[1] to 'people with chaotic lives and multiple needs' (HM Government, 2006a) – but the assumption that 'they' are different from the rest of us (and therefore require a new approach) is easily accompanied by perceiving them all as essentially similar. Ironically, this kind of 'othering' is evident even in an action plan to counter social exclusion (HM Government, 2006a). The families we interviewed had a wide range of experiences, strengths and difficulties. Some certainly had 'multiple and entrenched problems' but, in each case, the history, context and meaning of them was unique, and across the range of families there were as many similarities as differences.

One of the tensions or contradictions in current policy, then, is between the goal of a holistic approach to early intervention with families and the reliance on risk-factor checklists that require fairly minimal information. A second is between the duty to promote children's well-being, which is now placed on local authorities and other agencies working with them, and the anticipated failure of central government to reduce child poverty sufficiently to meet its targets. The many ways in which poverty could directly undermine children's well-being that were apparent in our study are summarised briefly in Chapter 5. Children are also of course affected by the impacts of poverty (among many other sources of adversity) on their parents, in a wide variety of ways that thread throughout this report. Perhaps most striking was the extent to which children as young as five worried about their parents' stress and often blamed themselves for it. They were also often distressed by siblings' behaviour problems. Promoting children's well-being requires a whole-family approach that also keeps in mind the needs of each individual member and the potential or actual conflicts between them. Reducing child poverty also requires a flexible approach to the role of paid work, since the impacts of parents' return to work on children's well-being are mixed and variable (Ridge, 2006).

A third tension is between the language of 'support for parents' and the parallel agenda of enforcing parental responsibilities. Linking rights to responsibilities has been an explicit theme throughout the current government, of course. The balance requires careful monitoring, however, if it is not to tip towards the latter to an extent that undermines policy intentions (and sometimes also human rights). For example, if schools are to become the base for a wide range of support services for parents, it may not be helpful that they are about to acquire the power to apply for parenting orders, especially since these are now to require only 'serious misbehaviour' on the child's part, not even exclusion from school, let alone criminal activity. Schools may well be wary of using these powers but, if they do and word gets round the local community, parents' fears of exposing their difficulties with their children in a school context may be increased. Using cuts to housing benefit as a sanction against parents for their anti-social behaviour also risks punishing and alienating their children too.

Another example is the changes to the tax credit system intended to help lift families on low incomes out of poverty. Increases in disregards and limits on recovery of overpayments are welcome changes. The responsibility 'pay-back', however, is reducing the time frame for the reporting of changes of relationship status from three months to one month (HM Treasury/DfES, 2005). This seems to require a high standard of decisiveness and organisation at a time of major change. Relationship breakdown is often distressing and full of conflict, repartnering is often uncertain and both may be unevenly paced between the two parties concerned. One month to agree and remember to report changes would be challenging for many people in comfortable circumstances. Those making policy might do well to consider if they would easily meet this standard themselves – before it is imposed on people whose lives are much more uncertain and constrained at the best of times. Setting the responsibility standard higher carries the risk of more people falling foul of it, and becoming alienated and excluded in the process.

A third example is the way the language of 'persistence' (sometimes accompanied by 'grip') is spreading from its use in intensive family support schemes with families with severe problems, usually including anti-social behaviour (such as the Dundee model), to become central to work with other 'hard-to-reach' families. Reminiscent of a police officer's hand around the arm of an offender, it implies control as much as if not more than care (although clearly it is meant to combine both). An alternative model, developed by ATD Fourth World (2006) and based much more on care, advocates a slow-moving approach, proactive but patient and flexible, enabling people with many disadvantages, fears and poor experiences of services to begin to build some trust and engage at their own pace.

There are many excellent intentions and promising initiatives in current policy. Earlier intervention, if it can be offered in a way acceptable to parents, is clearly what many want. Alongside innovative demonstration and pilot projects, however, more attention needs to be given to to the core institutional structures, e.g. the organisation of GP practices, and professions, e.g. recruitment and retention of social workers. Across all those working with families in poverty, more awareness of the impacts of poverty – its diverse social as well as material dimensions – is also needed to ensure that all are treated with respect and the contexts of their lives recognised.

Recommendations specific to different service areas are given below.

1. CENTRAL GOVERNMENT

Reducing child poverty – work, benefits and tax credits

- The report *Delivering on Child Poverty: What would it take?* (Harker, 2006) makes a series of recommendations to facilitate more parents working in jobs that lift them out of poverty in a sustainable way and to raise the incomes of those not working, including by increasing benefit levels. We urge the government to act on them.

- In addition, some specific changes to the benefits and tax credits systems are needed, including: (i) eligibility for passported benefits (such as free school meals) and social fund grants should remain open to those who are in work but whose income remains under a predetermined threshold; (ii) the potential gains from work income should not be undermined by the reduction or loss of housing benefit and council tax benefit. These are both important contributors to the conclusions parents reach that working is not worth it.

- Eligibility for the social fund should also be extended to those out of work who are on benefits other than income support (e.g. incapacity benefit, disability living allowance and carer's allowance, and contribution-based jobseeker's allowance – see Legge *et al.*, 2006).

- A regular start of school grants system should be added to the social fund to help those on low incomes with school-related costs, including school uniforms (Legge *et al.*, 2006). At present, local authorities make variable provision for school uniforms, but their obligation relates only to the time when children change schools from primary to secondary. Children need new uniforms as they grow, and inability to afford them contributes significantly to social exclusion and the risk of bullying. A stronger obligation should also be placed on local authorities to ensure that school uniforms are affordable. They could then achieve this by more grants and/or by introducing low-cost alternatives, e.g. a logo that could be attached to cheaper versions of an outfit that was similar to the uniform.

- Childcare from friends and family should be eligible for subsidy under the tax credit scheme, to allow parents to make use of childcare that may be more available and acceptable to them than formal arrangements. While family members can become registered childminders at present, if they provide care for at least one other child, there are costs to registering, and some may prefer not to submit family relationships to formal regulation.

- Access to advice on benefits and tax credits needs to be improved, with consideration given to making it available in locations that parents already go to (e.g. GP surgeries) or via practitioners they already see (e.g. health visitors). There are initiatives of this kind beginning, which should be extended. Application forms also need to be simplified.

- Access to help with budgeting and managing debt needs to be increased, including free legal advice. A limit to the interest that can legally be charged for loans should be introduced to reduce debt and its escalation.

Housing

- There is an urgent need for more investment in low-cost housing, especially in London, to address issues of overcrowding and inappropriate temporary accommodation. There is also a need for much greater investment to deal with problems with existing housing (e.g. cockroaches, damp, infestations of insects, broken fixtures, ill-fitting windows, no central heating) if the government is to meet its target that all social rented homes should reach the 'decent homes standard' by 2010.

Education

- More flexibility is needed in the curriculum to enable schools to plan for the needs of all children.

(Continued)

Health and social care

- Children who have been abused should have a right to therapeutic help within three months at most of when they seek it and services should be resourced sufficiently to guarantee this. This could significantly improve children's well-being, enhance their ability to achieve their full potential, and contribute to the prevention of anti-social behaviour, mental health problems and teenage pregnancy.

2. ALL AGENCIES WITH RESPONSIBILITY FOR CHILDREN'S WELL-BEING AT A LOCAL STRATEGIC PARTNERSHIP LEVEL

- The new duties that local authorities are acquiring with respect to information on childcare and other services for families mean information is now being compiled. Attention is needed to how to distribute it to ensure that it goes to all families, including those with little contact with services (other than a GP or possibly health visitor) and no internet access.

- One-stop shops and call centres should have freephone numbers to ensure that use is not prohibited by cost.

- More services that go into people's homes are needed to reach the most vulnerable parents in need of support and/or to develop creative ways of engaging parents (see ATD Fourth World, 2006 for an example). This is especially important for parents with mental health problems who may lack the energy, motivation or confidence to approach services themselves.

- More services are needed to support parents with older children, particularly in relation to managing emotional and behavioural problems. Those working with parents in all contexts need to be able to offer advice and information, including about further help available. Mentoring schemes for parents and the use of specially trained foster carers to offer respite to the rest of the family would be helpful.

- Planning for services to promote children's well-being should include attention to the availability and quality of low-cost housing. The impact of poor housing on parents' and children's well-being is under-recognised and at present this is not routinely incorporated.

- Improved access to affordable childcare is needed, not only to enable parents to work, but also for respite and relief from childcare responsibilities for parents who are not working but are under particular stress.

- The many sources of stigma that may inhibit use of services need to be countered with public information, e.g. mental health problems, including in the Bangladeshi community.

- All services need to consider how to meet childcare needs, assist with the cost of them and/or take account of childcare responsibilities.

- Access to cheaper or free public transport needs to be increased for low-income families (following the example of London).

- Interpretation services should be widely available, as should information for families in all languages, in all services.

- The importance of continuity of workers for families needs to be appreciated, both by addressing retention problems and by dealing with necessary endings with care.

- Free and accessible facilities and activities for children living on low incomes need to be increased, in all community contexts. Public spaces such as parks, playgrounds and sports facilities need to be better maintained, and in some contexts supervised to ensure children are not intimidated away from using them by local gangs.

(Continued)

- Relatively affluent areas need to give particular consideration to how to ensure low-income families have access to services and amenities (e.g. through extending help with transport and childcare where services are at some distance).

3. LOCAL AUTHORITIES – HOUSING DEPARTMENTS

- The response of housing departments to families, particularly in London, has to be improved. Systems need to be in place to provide quicker and more efficient responses to families experiencing problems with housing. Acknowledgement of problems and communication with families with regard to their housing position would be a basic yet much appreciated step.

- There needs to be more access to free legal advice and advocacy support for families regarding housing issues in order to help those who are less able to fight for change.

4. PROVIDERS OF HEALTH SERVICES

- GPs need to have access to information about local support services that they can recommend/refer families to. This is particularly important for those families with mental health problems/minority ethnic families who may only ever visit the GP.

- Consideration needs also to be given to extending the role of GPs in child protection to prevention, for example, through voluntary screening for problems such as domestic violence and drug and alcohol abuse for which parents can be referred to appropriate services for help.

- The use of GP surgeries as bases for co-located services and/or information and advice for families, including information relevant to low-income families, and leaflets or posters that counter stigma and encourage help-seeking in relation to a range of problems, should be considered.

- Midwives/ante-natal care are now expected routinely to screen for domestic violence. They should also provide space for the experience of rape (by a partner or by someone else) to be explored. This would help to identify at an early stage women who were pregnant as a result of rape and provide them with the appropriate support.

- Resources for health visiting need to be increased and training for health visitors provided to enable them to help parents whose children have developed behaviour problems.

- The value of continuity of relationship between patient/parent and GP/health visitor needs to be appreciated – structures for allocation should facilitate continuity where possible.

- GPs and health visitors need to act more quickly to respond to mental health problems among parents, including diagnosis and referral, to prevent harm to children when problems escalate.

- Access to counselling/therapeutic services for children and parents needs to be radically improved, with waiting times made much shorter than at present. A range of approaches need to be available, with flexibility over timing to allow people to seek help when they need it and for as long as they need it.

(Continued)

- An information pack should be made available to all those suffering from mental health problems when they are prescribed anti-depressants – to include information about the nature and frequency of mental health problems, the possible impact on other family members and other sources of help (including self-help groups) and self-help advice.

- Public education around mental health should seek particularly to address the stigma attached to mental health problems in minority ethnic communities.

5. LOCAL EDUCATION AUTHORITIES AND SCHOOLS

- Care needs to be taken in communications over extra activities with costs that parents on low incomes are not intimidated or embarrassed if the costs, however small, are beyond their budget.

- More subsidies are needed for school trips, etc. to enable all children to participate. Existing subsidies for low-income families should be extended beyond those on income support to all those up to a certain income level (e.g. by giving parents the option to give information about receipt of working tax credit).

- The distance requirements for eligibility for transport subsidies to and from school need to be revised (currently, children under eight are eligible only if they live more than two miles away and children over eight if they live more than three miles away). Since children walk to school much less frequently than they used to, this can create substantial time and financial costs for parents.

- Schools need to ensure that they communicate clearly with parents when problems arise at school with children, both explaining their concerns and listening to the parents' experience of their children.

- Improved advice/support is needed for parents whose children have emotional and behavioural difficulties and around the process of children receiving a statement of special educational need.

- Information, support and advocacy for parents whose children have special needs or emotional and behavioural difficulties is provided by some local authorities in a range of ways. It needs to be available in all areas, whether by LA parent advice centres or partnership with voluntary sector organisations.

- Training on child protection issues for teachers should explore the circumstances in which communicating with parents about a referral can safely be done.

- Training should also increase teachers' understanding of the pressures faced by families living in poverty, and the implications for both teaching children and engaging with parents.

- Homework clubs need to be available in all areas to ensure children have help with homework when their parents are unable to provide it.

- Children under stress at home should have easy access themselves within schools to support, including counselling, advocacy and referral to other services.

6. PROVIDERS OF CHILDREN'S SERVICES

- A more holistic approach is needed to working with families. Both anti-oppressive practice and an ecological framework require social workers to have a fuller appreciation of the many ways poverty impacts on family life. Many parents also have histories of and/or ongoing abuse, violence and trauma in their own lives, and need support for their own needs alongside intervention on their children's behalf. More recognition is also needed of the impact of children with serious behaviour problems on their parents and siblings, and appropriate help should be offered to manage and reduce it.

- More attention is also needed to the emotional dynamics of the interactions between parents and social workers, both in training and by the provision of sufficient ongoing supervision to enable social workers to manage the emotional impacts of their work.

- Clearer communication with families is needed around social services intervention. Parents' anxieties need to be reduced sufficiently to enable them to explain their circumstances fully at investigation and assessment. Written information needs also to be provided, especially in relation to the reasons for registration and what can be expected after it from their social worker and others, so that they can refer back to it when they need to, to alleviate any confusion or uncertainty.

- Social workers need access to a regularly updated directory of national and local support services for low-income families, those with parenting problems and a range of associated issues (e.g. domestic violence, rape, mental health problems, drug and alcohol abuse) to refer families on to.

- They also need accurate information about what financial help families can receive from where, including organisations they can apply to for financial and practical help on behalf of families where it is not available from SS.

- More information needs to be made available to families about children's disabilities – families need to have information about the nature of the disability/illness, how they can support their children and best meet their needs, and how children's needs are likely to change over time.

- Continuity of workers for families is a particular problem and retention difficulties need to be addressed.

- More resources need to be made available to meet identified need.

7. TRAINING BODIES

- All organisations providing training for professionals working with parents, especially for social workers and health visitors, need to pay more attention to the many and complex ways in which poverty impacts on family life – appreciation of these is essential if practitioners are to engage families on low incomes in service provision and alleviate rather than increase social exclusion. The National Academy for Parenting Professionals may have a significant role to play here.

- Training also needs to help professionals to engage with young children and listen to their views, both in the context of safeguarding children and in family courts. The tendency to regard 12 as the age at which children are able to judge their own interests may leave younger children at significant risk.

8. FAMILY COURTS

> • The views of all children, including those under the age of 12, should be given due consideration in disputes over contact and residence.

9. THE CRIMINAL JUSTICE SYSTEM

> • Care needs to be taken to explain, both to parents and (in age-appropriate ways) to children, why cases involving child maltreatment are dropped or defendants acquitted.

NOTE

1. This phrase was used in the DfES/HM Treasury call for evidence for the Joint Policy Review on Children and Young People, dated 2 August 2006, and picked up subsequently by the press – see, for example, *The Guardian*, 6 September 2006.

References

ATD Fourth World (2006) *Not too Hard to Reach: Developing a tool to reach the most disadvantaged families*. London: ATD Fourth World.

Atkinson, R. and Kintrea, K. (2001) 'Disentangling area effects: evidence from deprived and non-deprived neighbourhoods'. *Urban Studies*, 38 (12), 2277–98.

Atkinson, R. and Kintrea, K. (2004) '"Opportunities and despair, it's all in there": practitioner experiences and explanations of area effects and life chances'. *Sociology*, 38 (3), 437–55.

Attree, P. (2004) *Parenting in Disadvantage – a Meta-synthesis of the Qualitative Evidence*. Lancaster: Institute for Health Research, Lancaster University.

Baginsky, M. (2003) *Responsibility without Power? Local education authorities and child protection*. London: NSPCC.

Baginsky, M. (2006) *Responding to Change – a Survey of Local Education Authorities' Responses to the Changing Policy Context of Child Protection*. London: NSPCC

Bailey, N. (2006) 'Does work pay? Employment, poverty and exclusion from social relations', in C. Pantazis, D. Gordon and R. Levitas (eds), *Poverty and Social Exclusion in Britain: The Millennium Survey*. London: Policy Press.

Barnes, J., Baylis. G., Hill, S., Jalil, N., Pitt, C., Quinn, D. and Woodrow, J. (no date) 'Place and parenting: the Families and Neighbourhoods Study: summary of interview findings, Unpublished paper, Institute for the Study of Children, Families and Social Issues, Birkbeck, University of London.

Barnes, J. and Cheng, H. (2006) 'Do parental neighbourhood perceptions contribute to child behaviour problems? A study of disadvantaged children'. *Vulnerable Children and Youth Studies*, 1 (1), 2–14.

Barry, M. (2006) *Youth Offending in Transition: The search for social recognition*. London: Routledge.

Batchelor, S. (2005) '" Prove me the bam!" Victimisation and agency in the lives of young women who commit violent offences'. *Probation Journal*, 52 (4), 358–75.

Baumrind, D. (1967) 'Childcare practices anteceding three patterns of preschool behaviour'. *Genetic Psychology Monographs*, 75 (1), 43–88.

Benjamin, L. *et al.* (1998) 'The parenting experiences of mothers with dissociative disorders'. *Journal of Marital and Family Therapy*, 24 (3), 337–54.

Blandon, J. and Gibbons, S. (2006) *The Persistence of Poverty across the Generations: A view from two British cohorts*. London: The Policy Press.

Bradshaw, J. (2000) 'Child poverty in comparative perspective', in D. Gordon and P. Townsend (eds), *Breadline Europe*. Bristol: Policy Press.

Bradshaw, J. (ed.) (2002) *The Well-being of Children in the UK*. London: Save the Children/University of York.

Bradshaw, J. and Mayhew, E. (eds) (2005) *The Well-being of Children in the UK 2005 (Volume 2)*. London: Save the Children/University of York.

Bronfenbrenner, U. (1979) *The Ecology of Human Development*. Cambridge, MA: Harvard University Press.

Brown, G. and Harris, T. (1978) *Social Origins of Depression: A study of psychiatric disorder in women*. London: Tavistock.

Cawson, P., Wattam, C., Brooker, S. and Kelly, G. (2000) *Child Maltreatment in the United Kingdom: A study of the prevalence of abuse and neglect*. London: NSPCC.

Connolly, M., Crichton-Hill, Y. and Ward, T. (eds) (2006) *Culture and Child Protection: Reflexive responses*. London: Jessica Kingsley.

Cooper, A. and Lousada, J. (2005) *Borderline Welfare: Feeling and fear of feeling in modern welfare*. Tavistock Clinic Series. London: Karnac Books.

Crittenden, P.M. (1999) 'Child neglect: causes and contributors', in H. Dubowitz (ed.), *Neglected Children: Research, practice and policy*. Thousand Oaks, CA: Sage.

Crowley, A. and Vulliamy, C. (2002) *Listen Up! Children and young people talk about poverty*. London: Save the Children.

CSCI (Commission for Social Care Inspection) (2006) *Supporting Parents, Safeguarding Children: Meeting the needs of parents on the Child Protection Register*. London: CSCI.

Daniel, B. (2006) 'Operationalising resilience: emergent issues'. Paper presented at ISPCAN Conference, *Children in a Changing World: Getting it right*, York, September.

Datamonitor (2006) *Western European Consumer Credit 2006*. London: Datamonitor.

Department of Health (1995) *Child Protection: Messages from research*. London: HMSO.

Department of Health (2002) *Women's Mental Health: Into the mainstream: Strategic development of mental health care for women*. London: Department of Health.

Department of Health, Department for Education and Employment and Home Office (2000) *Framework for the Assessment of Children in Need and their Families*. London: HMSO.

DiLeonardi, J.W. (1993) 'Families in poverty and chronic neglect of children'. *Families in Society*, 74 (9), 557–62.

Drake, B. and Pandey, S. (1996) 'Understanding the relationship between neighbourhood poverty and specific types of child maltreatment'. *Child Abuse and Neglect*, 20 (11), 1103–18.

Dubowitz, H. (2006) 'Confronting child neglect: concepts and challenges'. Paper presented at ISPCAN Conference, *Children in a Changing World: Getting it right*, York, September.

Duncan, G.J. and Brooks-Gunn, J. (1997) 'Income effects across the life span: integration and interpretation', in G.J. Duncan and J. Brooks-Gunn (eds), *Consequences of Growing up Poor*. New York: Russell Sage Foundation.

Duncan, G.J., Brooks-Gunn, J. and Klebanov, P.K. (1994) 'Economic deprivation and early-childhood development', *Child Development*, 65, 296–318.

DWP (Department for Work and Pensions) (2006) *Opportunity for All: 8th annual report*. London: DWP.

Edleson, J.L. (2001) 'Studying the co-occurrence of child maltreatment and women battering in families', in S.A. Graham-Bermann and J.L. Edleson (eds), *Domestic Violence in the Lives of Children: The future of research*. Washington, DC: American Psychological Association.

Egeland, B. (1993) 'A history of abuse is a major risk factor for abusing the next generation', in R.J. Gelles and D.R. Loseke (eds), *Current Controversies on Family Violence*. Newbury Park, CA: London: Sage.

Egeland, B. and Susman-Stillman, A. (1996) 'Dissociation as a mediator of child abuse across generations'. *Child Abuse and Neglect*, 20 (11), 1123–32.

Fitzpatrick, S. (2004) *Poverty of Place*. Working paper. York: Centre for Housing Policy, University of York.

Fontes, L.A. (2005) *Child Abuse and Culture: Working with diverse families*. New York: Guilford.

Fraser, N. (1997) *Justice Interruptus: Critical reflections on the 'postsocialist' condition*. New York and London: Routledge.

Gelles, R.J. (1987) *Family Violence*. Thousand Oaks, CA: Sage.

Gest, S.D., Sesma Jr, A., Masten, A.S. and Tellegen, A. (2006) 'Childhood peer reputation as a predictor of competence and symptoms 10 years later'. *Journal of Abnormal Child Psychology*, 34 (4), 509–26.

Ghate, D. and Hazel, N. (2002) *Parenting in Poor Environments: Stress, support and coping.* London: Jessica Kingsley Publishers.

Giddens, A. (1998) *The Third Way: The renewal of social democracy.* Cambridge: Polity Press.

Gillham, B., Tanner, G., Cheyne, B., Freeman, I., Rooney, M. and Lambie, A. (1998) 'Unemployment rates, single parent density and indices of child poverty: their relationship to different categories of child abuse and neglect'. *Child Abuse and Neglect*, 22, 79–90.

Gilligan, R. (2004) 'Promoting resilience in child and family social work: issues for social work practice, education and policy'. *Journal of Social Work Education*, 23 (1), 93–104.

Gilligan, R. (2006) 'Promoting resilience and permanence in child welfare', in J. Barber, P. Dudding and R. Flynn (eds), *Promoting Resilient Development in Children Receiving Care.* Ottawa: University of Ottawa Press.

Goodman, R. (1997) 'The Strengths and Difficulties Questionnaire: a research note'. *Journal of Child Psychology and Psychiatry*, 38 (5), 581–6.

Gordon, D., Levitas, R. and Pantazis, C. (2006) *Poverty and Social Exclusion in Britain: The Millennium Survey.* London: Policy Press.

Gorin, S. (2004) *Understanding What Children Say. Children's experiences of domestic violence, parental substance misuse and parental health problems.* London: National Children's Bureau on behalf of JRF.

Hakim, C. (2000) *Work–lifestyle Choices in the 21st Century: Preference theory.* Oxford: Oxford University Press.

Hanmer, J. and Itzin, C. (eds) (2001) *Home Truths about Domestic Violence: Feminist influences on policy and practice: A reader.* London: Routledge

Hao, L. and Matsueda, R.L. (2006) 'Family dynamics through childhood: a sibling model of behaviour problems'. *Social Science Research*, 35, 500–24.

Harker, L. (2006) *Delivering on Child Poverty: What would it take? A report for the Department of Work and Pensions.* Cm. 6951. London: HMSO.

Heard, D.H. and Lake, B. (1986) 'The attachment dynamic in adult life'. *British Journal of Psychiatry*, 149, 430–8.

Heard, D. and Lake, B. (1997) *The Challenge of Attachment for Caregiving.* London: Routledge.

Herman, J. (1992) *Trauma and Recovery.* New York: Basic Books.

Hirsch, D. (2006) *What Will it Take to End Child Poverty? Firing on all cylinders.* York: Joseph Rowntree Foundation.

HM Government (2004) *Every Child Matters: Change for children*. London: HMSO.

HM Government (2006a) *Reaching out: An action plan for social exclusion*. London: HMSO.

HM Government (2006b) *Working Together to Safeguard Children: A guide to inter-agency working to safeguard and promote the welfare of children*. London: TSO.

HM Treasury/DfES (2005) *Support for Parents: The best start for children*. London: HMSO.

Hoggett, P. (2000) *Emotional Life and the Politics of Welfare*. London: Macmillan/St Martin's Press.

Hollway, W. and Jefferson, T. (2000) *Doing Qualitative Research Differently: Free association, narrative and the interview method*. London: Sage.

Home Office (2006) *Respect Action Plan*. London: Respect Task Force, Home Office.

Hooper, C. (2003) *Abuse, Interventions and Women in Prison: A literature review*. London: Home Office/HM Prison Service.

Jack, G. (2000) 'Ecological influences on parenting and child development'. *British Journal of Social Work*, 30, 703–20.

Jack, G. (2004) 'Child protection at the community level'. *Child Abuse Review*, 13, 368–83.

Jack, G. (2006) 'The area and community components of children's well-being'. *Children and Society*, 20, 334–47.

Jewell, S. (2006) 'Children give safety top priority'. *The Guardian*, 11 October.

Katz, I. (2004) 'Poverty, social exclusion and child abuse'. Unpublished paper for the NSPCC, London.

Katz, I., Corlyon, J., La Placa, V. and Hunter, S. (2007, forthcoming) *The Relationship Between Parenting and Poverty*. York: Joseph Rowntree Foundation.

Kaufman, J. and Zigler, E. (1993) 'The intergenerational transmission of abuse is overstated', in R.J. Gelles and D.R. Loseke (eds), *Current Controversies on Family Violence*. Newbury Park, CA/London: Sage.

Kiernan, K. (2006) 'Partnership and parenthood'. Paper presented at National Parenting and Family Institute, *Parent and Child Conference 2006*, London, November.

Knight, A., Chase, E. and Aggleton, P. (2006) 'Someone of your own to love: experiences of being looked after as influences on teenage pregnancy'. *Children and Society*, 20, 391–403.

Lau, A.S., Valeri, S.M., McCarty, C.A. and Weisz, J.R. (2006) 'Abusive parents' reports of child behaviour problems: relationship to observed parent–child interactions'. *Child Abuse and Neglect*, 30, 639–55.

Layard, R. (2005) *Happiness: Lessons from a new science*. London: Penguin.

Legge, K., Hartfree, Y., Stafford, B., Magadi, M., Beckhelling, J., Predelli, L.N. and Middleton, S. (2006) *The Social Fund: Current role and future direction*. York: Joseph Rowntree Foundation.

Levitas, R. (2006) 'The concept and measurement of social exclusion', in C. Pantazis, D. Gordon and R. Levitas (eds), *Poverty and Social Exclusion in Britain: The Millennium Survey*. London: Policy Press.

Lister, R. (2004) *Poverty*. Cambridge: Polity Press.

Lovell, C.H. (1992) *Breaking the Cycle of Poverty: The BRAC Strategy*. Bloomfield, CT: Kumarian Press.

McCluskey, U. (2005) *To Be Met as a Person: The dynamics of attachment in professional encounters*. London: Karnac.

McDermott, E., Graham, H. and Hamilton, V. (2004) *Experiences of Being a Teenage Mother in the UK: A report of a systematic review of qualitative studies*. Glasgow: ESRC Centre for Evidence-based Public Policy, Social and Public Health Services Unit, University of Glasgow.

McGuigan, W.M. and Pratt, C.C. (2001) 'The predictive impact of domestic violence on three types of child maltreatment'. *Child Abuse and Neglect*, 25, 869–83.

Madge, N. (2006) *Children These Days*. Bristol: Policy Press.

Marjolin, N. (2005) *Respect to Protect Project Report, Internal Evaluation*. London: NSPCC.

Marris, P. (1996) *The Politics of Uncertainty: Attachment in private and public life*. London: Routledge.

Masten, A.S., Roisman, G.I., Long, J.D., Burt, K.B., Obradovic, J., Riley, J.R., Boelcke-Stennes, K. and Tellegen, A. (2005) 'Developmental cascades: linking academic achievement and externalising and internalising symptoms over 20 years'. *Developmental Psychology*, 41 (5), 733–46.

Mullender, A. (1996) *Rethinking Domestic Violence: The social work and probation response*. London: Routledge.

National Commission of Inquiry into the Prevention of Child Abuse (1996) *Childhood Matters: Report of the National Commission of Inquiry into the Prevention of Child Abuse: Vol. 1*. London: HMSO.

Pantazis, C. and Ruspini, E. (2006) 'Gender, poverty and social exclusion', in C. Pantazis, D. Gordon and R. Levitas (eds), *Poverty and Social Exclusion in Britain: The Millennium Survey*. London: Policy Press.

Park, A., Phillips, M. and Johnson, M. (2004) *Young People in Britain: The attitudes and experiences of 12 to 19 year olds*. London: DfES.

Pike, A., Coldwell, J. and Dunn, J. (2006) *Family Relationships in Middle Childhood*. London: National Children's Bureau.

Radford, L. and Hester, M. (2006) *Mothering through Domestic Violence*. London: Jessica Kingsley.

Rainey, D.Y., Stevens-Simon, C. and Kaplan, D.W. (1995) 'Are adolescents who report prior sexual abuse at higher risk for pregnancy'. *Child Abuse and Neglect*, 19 (12), 1283–8.

Reder, P. and Duncan, S. (2001) 'Abusive relationships, care and control conflicts and insecure attachments'. *Child Abuse Review*, 10 (6), 411–27.

Ridge, T. (2002) *Childhood Poverty and Social Exclusion: From a child's perspective*. Bristol: Policy Press.

Ridge, T. (2006) 'It's a family affair: children's perspectives on parental work'. Paper presented at the Social Policy Association Conference, University of Birmingham, 18–20 July.

Rosenthal, J.A. and Curiel, H.F. (2006) 'Modelling behavioural problems of children in the child welfare system: caregiver, youth and teacher perceptions'. *Children and Youth Services Review*, 28, 1392–408.

Ruscio, A.M. (2001) 'Predicting the child-rearing practices of mothers sexually abused in childhood'. *Child Abuse and Neglect*, 25, 369–87.

Rutter, M., Tizard, B. and Whitmore, W. (1970) *Education, Health and Behaviour*. London: Longman.

Seaman, P., Turner, K., Hill, M., Stafford, A. and Walker, M. (2005) *Parenting and Children's Resilience in Disadvantaged Communities*. London: National Children's Bureau, Joseph Rowntree Foundation.

Sheppard, M. (1994) 'Childcare, social support and maternal depression: a review and application of findings'. *British Journal of Social Work*, 24, 287–310.

Sheppard, M. (2001) *Social Work Practice with Depressed Mothers in Child and Family Care*. London: The Stationery Office.

Shropshire, J. and Middleton, S. (1999) *Small Expectations: Learning to be poor?* York: Joseph Rowntree Foundation.

Sidebotham, P. and Heron, J. (2006) 'Child maltreatment in the "children of the nineties": a cohort study of risk factors'. *Child Abuse and Neglect*, 30 (5), 497–522.

Sidebotham, P., Heron, J. and Golding, J. (2002) 'Child maltreatment in the "children in the nineties": deprivation, class and social networks in a UK sample'. *Child Abuse and Neglect*, 26 (2), 1243–59.

Silverthorn, P. and Frick, P.J. (1999) 'Developmental pathways to antisocial behaviour: the delayed-onset pathway in girls'. *Development and Psychopathology*, 11, 101–26.

Sternberg, K.J., Lamb, M.E., Guterman, E. and Abbott, C.B. (2006) 'Effects of early and later family violence on children's behaviour problems and depression: a longitudinal, multi-informant perspective'. *Child Abuse and Neglect*, 30, 283–306.

Townsend, P. (1979) *Poverty in the United Kingdom, a Survey of Household Resources and Standards of Living*. London: Penguin Books.

Tuck, V. (2000) 'Socio-economic factors: a neglected dimension in harm to children', in J. Botslear and B. Humphries (eds), *Welfare, Exclusion and Political Agency*. London: Routledge.

Unicef (2005) *Child Poverty in Rich Countries*. Innocenti Report Card No. 6. Florence: Unicef Innocenti Research Centre.

Weaver, M. (2006) '"Supernannies" to tackle antisocial children'. *The Guardian*, 21 November.

Wilkinson, R. (2005) *The Impact of Inequality*. New York: New Press.

Willow, C. (2002) *Participation in Practice. Children and young people as partners in change*. London: The Children's Society.

Zuravin, S., McMillen, C., DePanfilis, D. and Risley-Curtiss, C. (1996) 'The intergenerational cycle of child maltreatment'. *Journal of Interpersonal Violence*, 11 (3), 315–34.

For further information on child poverty visit www.endchildpoverty.org.uk who provide comprehensive information about the aspects and implications of child poverty and what needs to be done to eradicate it. End Child Poverty is a coalition of children's and other charities, social justice groups, faith-groups, trade unions and others campaigning together for change.

Index

Page numbers given in bold indicate figures in the report.